BBY MOORE · STUART PEARCE · BOB
RNES · PAUL GASCOIGN
BANKS · EDDIE HAPGO
VID BECKHAM · JOHN BARNES · PAU
ER · HARRY KANE · GORDON BANKS
RCE · BOBBY CHARLTON · DAVID BE
F HURST GARY LINEKER · HARRY K
BBY MOORE · STUART PEARCE · BOB
RNES · PAUL GASCOIGNE · GEOFF H
BANKS · EDDIE HAPGOOD · BOBBY
VID BECKHAM · JOHN BARNES · PAU
ER · HARRY KANE · GORDON BANKS
RCE · BOBBY CHARLTON · DAVID BE
F HURST GARY LINEKER · HARRY K
BBY MOORE · STUART PEARCE · BOB
RNES · PAUL GASCOIGNE · GEOFF H
BANKS · EDDIE HAPGOOD · BOBBY
VID BECKHAM · JOHN BARNES · PAU
ER · HARRY KANE · GORDON BANKS
RCE · BOBBY CHARLTON · DAVID BE
F HURST GARY LINEKER · HARRY K
BBY MOORE · STUART PEARCE · BOB

HOLSTEN

The IMMORTALS *of* English Football

English football's finest hour – Bobby Moore holds aloft the Jules Rimet Trophy during the lap of honour after the 1966 World Cup final, with team-mates Geoff Hurst, Gordon Banks and Roger Hunt joining the celebrations.

The IMMORTALS of English Football

Chris Bevan

GELDING STREET PRESS

A Gelding Street Press book
An imprint of Rockpool Publishing
PO Box 252
Summer Hill
NSW 2130 Australia

geldingstreetpress.com
Follow us! Geldingstreetpress

ISBN: 9781922662170

Published in 2025 by Gelding Street Press

Design and typesetting by Christine Armstrong, Rockpool Publishing
Edited by Brooke Halliwell

NATIONAL LIBRARY OF AUSTRALIA
A catalogue record for this book is available from the National Library of Australia

Printed and bound in China

10 9 8 7 6 5 4 3 2 1

DEDICATION

For Florence and Clara, with love

Gordon Banks jumps to punch clear a cross during England's opening game of the 1966 World Cup, a 0–0 draw against Uruguay. He played every minute of the campaign, keeping four clean sheets from six matches.

Contents

Four of England's Immortals, Gordon Banks, Geoff Hurst, Bobby Moore and Bobby Charlton, line up with the rest of the England team and pose with the Jules Rimet Trophy after winning the 1966 World Cup final.

INTRODUCTION

'The impossible job' is a phrase often used to describe managing the England national football team, but it is also appropriate for this daunting task of selecting 11 male players who have achieved Immortal status while wearing the Three Lions on their shirt.

Since their first international fixture, against Scotland, at Hamilton Crescent in Glasgow in November 1872, the England men's team have played over 1,000 games, using more than 1,250 players.

That clearly gives me plenty to choose from here, but also lots to be left out – so, which of them qualify as Immortals, and who else even comes close?

First and foremost, as the basis for this book, the term 'Immortals' itself needs some context and explanation.

Borrowed from other sports, it is the practice of honouring a select group of players who are regarded as enduring examples of the game's absolute elite, but Immortals in this sense are not just England's most talented players, or highest achievers.

I would define them as influential individuals who set standards on and off the pitch, and helped change the way their sport was played or viewed across wider society, often dealing with the prejudices of their time along the way.

I have tried to recognise various different historical periods, but the game, and the way it is enjoyed and analysed, has changed immeasurably during the past 150 years, so any comparisons across eras are always difficult and often impossible to make.

What it is plausible to do down the decades is gauge the impact that different individuals have had on the England team, English football and the English public as a whole, through their prodigious talent but also through their competitive success, spirit, character and fame, and reflect on their legacy based on their achievements with all of those factors combined.

Of course numbers can help us to recognise the greats but, with a far greater number of international games played now than there were in the past, I did not want this to be an exercise in statistics alone that merely celebrated the most capped players through the ages – although the all-time highest scorers did demand rather more consideration.

Trophies cannot be ignored either, but the obvious issue with using them here as a barometer of individual excellence is that the Three Lions have only ever won one major international tournament, the 1966 World Cup.

Still, it is that success and the many failed attempts to repeat it that have shaped the story of England's football team so far and will doubtless continue to do so in the future.

Major finals seem uniquely able to unite this nation in joy and, more often, despair, so it feels right that feats on that stage are used as a key influence in measuring a player's qualifications for inclusion as an Immortal.

It is not the only yardstick, however, especially because England did not even enter a team in a World Cup until 1950 or the European Championship until 1964. I did not want to ignore the many amazing feats of the players who came before then, during times when truly international football either did not exist or was not properly recognised on these shores.

It was important to settle on some consistent criteria, however, whichever era is considered. All players past and present were chosen for their impact and legacy for England over their achievements and success for their clubs, but it was impossible to ignore that part of their careers and would be wrong to overlook how it helped to shape their lives and build their reputations.

Also, there are 11 players included because one of my aims was to form a functioning team – well, actually a formidable one – although there were various reasons I did not enforce any specific roles, such as right-back or holding midfielder, to be filled.

The game has not always used the same terms to describe players who do a similar job and, in any case, they often don't reflect where the player ends up operating.

More importantly, England's ever-changing formation as the game has evolved tactically over time means they have not always used all of the same positions either.

Take, for example, the difference between Sir Alf Ramsey's wingless

Paul Gascoigne's heroics at the 1990 World Cup and 1996 European Championship won him a place in the nation's hearts.

wonders who won the 1966 World Cup, Sir Bobby Robson's sweeper system in the same tournament in 1990 and Terry Venables' 'Christmas Tree' shape that came so close in the 1996 European Championships.

I felt no-one should be excluded here on the basis they don't fit into the shape of my team or, equally, picked because I needed to fill a specialist position so, instead, I have kept that side of it relatively simple. As well as a goalkeeper, I have chosen three defenders, four midfielders and three forwards.

This would be an extremely attack-minded side if it were possible for it to line up together on a pitch, but is also a team full of the kind of flair and fight that has defined England during their most memorable moments.

Those attributes actually emerged as important elements for all the players included, as did their drive to succeed.

'Safe as the Banks of England' – Gordon Banks collects the ball over another of England's Immortals, Bobby Moore.

While several of them could be described as 'naturally' gifted, it was striking how hard work and a determination to be the best made the difference for so many who are now remembered as legends of the game – an important lesson, perhaps, for anyone attempting to follow in their footsteps.

Some of those chosen had flaws too, making mistakes which sometimes led to the heartbreak and humiliation that has undermined so many of our bids for glory, but that was just another part of their journey, and it is their response and redemption for those setbacks that is recognised here.

There are many ups and downs as this book explores the lives and careers of each of the 11 players, but I wanted to pay particular attention to the moment or moments that make them true England greats, and I've attempted to analyse why they have played such a special part in their country's footballing history. In some cases, there is hopefully more to come.

For the record, there are no female England players included here – the women's game is already compared to the men's far too much, and their Immortals deserve their own recognition independently. Also, just choosing 11 men alone was hard enough, as anyone attempting it would no doubt agree.

I am sure you will have your own ideas about who should have been included but then no list like this should fail to provoke discussion, debate and even controversy.

I hope you enjoy my selections, and their stories, even if you don't agree with my final team or my suggestions about who would be left on the bench.

Chris Bevan
August 2024

Gordon Banks was voted Football Writers' Footballer of the Year in 1972 and won FIFA's Goalkeeper of the Year award every year between 1966 and 1971.

1

Gordon Banks

Born	30 December 1937; died 12 February 2019
Place of birth	Abbeydale, Sheffield
Position	Goalkeeper

Gordon Banks played 73 games in goal for England between 1963 and 1972, conceding 57 goals and keeping 35 clean sheets. He was on the losing side on only nine occasions and played in 23 consecutive games between 1964 and 1967 without defeat, including the 1966 World Cup final. His friend Pelé called him 'a goalkeeper with magic' and 'a fine human being'.

Where to start? In goal, where else. England has produced many fine goalkeepers down the years, but the choice here was actually quite an easy one.

Gordon Banks became a legend on home soil when he played a key role in winning the World Cup at Wembley in 1966 but the defining moment of his career took place four years later and thousands of miles away, when he entered footballing folklore and earned global fame by denying arguably the greatest player of all time in truly astonishing fashion, with what many believe is the best save they have ever seen.

The scene is the Estadio Jalisco in Guadalajara, Mexico, on 7 June 1970, as England's defence of their title sees them face the might of pre-tournament favourites Brazil in the group stage.

The game is just 10 minutes old when Jairzinho lopes on to Carlos Alberto's incredible swerving pass, bursts past Terry Cooper down the right wing and stands up a looping, hanging cross to the back post, where it is met by a galloping Pelé, who leaps high above Tommy Wright and powers his header downwards, sending the ball bouncing towards what appears to be an empty corner of the net.

It is goalbound in every sense of the word, until a blue-shirted figure – Banks, whose starting position was on the other side of the goal – hurtles across and launches himself horizontally to somehow get something, and whether it's a finger or hand, it's enough, in the way to brilliantly turn the rising ball over the bar.

'The moment the ball left his head, I heard Pelé shout "Golo!",' Banks wrote in his 2002 autobiography. 'Faced with a situation like that, you don't have time to think.'

'All my experience and technique took over. I suddenly found myself at a forty-degree angle with my right hand stretching out towards the post, my eyes trained on the quickly descending ball.

'One thing did flash through my mind: If I do make contact, I'll not hold this. The ball hit the ground two yards in front of me but I managed to make contact with the finger of my gloved right hand and I was able to scoop it high into the air.

'I landed crumpled against the inner side netting of the goal, and my first reaction was to look at Pelé. I hadn't a clue where the ball was. He had ground to a halt, head clasped between his hands and I knew then all I needed to know.'

Watching the save back now, like many millions have on YouTube, it appears to be football from a different world, let alone a distant era. The 1970 World Cup was the first to be televised live in colour and the grainy footage combined with, by modern standards, poor camerawork only enhances the magic of Banks's agility and elegance.

The angle of the coverage is so close up that the goalkeeper is not in shot as Pelé dashes in to head the ball goalwards. When Banks suddenly flies into view, you are left shaking your head in disbelief at what you have just seen. You won't be the only one.

'I hit that header exactly as I'd hoped,' Pelé said later. 'Exactly where I wanted it to go. I was ready to celebrate but then this man, Banks, appeared in my sight, like a kind of blue phantom, is how I described him.

'He came from nowhere and he did something I didn't

Banks made his England debut in a 2–1 defeat against Scotland in 1963.

feel was possible. He pushed my header, somehow, up and over. I couldn't believe what I saw. Even now, when I watch it, I can't believe it. I can't believe how he moved so far, so fast.'

Pelé, ever the sportsman, congratulated Banks almost immediately. For the viewers back home, legendary BBC commentator David Coleman summed it up perfectly: 'What a save, Gordon Banks. He picked that out of the net. That's the save of the World Cup – how that one came back, even Banks won't know – pure reaction, and pure brilliance.'

Banks initially described the save as 'lucky' but he was given plenty of opportunities to analyse it properly, as his World Cup winning team-mate Geoff Hurst explained when he included Banks in the list of his 50 all-time finest footballers in 2014.

'Whenever people meet Gordon the first thing they ask him about is that save and it always raises a smile to see him respond,' Hurst wrote.

'Almost without fail he'll give a withering sigh and mutter something along the lines of "I'm fed up of people talking about that save, that's all they ever want to know about". . . before quickly perking up and saying "but I'll

'. . . how that one came back, even Banks won't know – pure reaction, and pure brilliance.'
– David Coleman

talk you through it." It's a story he loves telling, and so he should.'

Out of the dozens of vital stops that Banks made for his country, it is the one he is always remembered for. As he would always say himself, he is more famous for that one moment than for winning the World Cup.

Banks helped Stoke City beat Chelsea 2–1 in the 1972 League Cup final.

Rather than luck, it was only possible because of the countless extra hours Banks spent on the training ground over the course of his career after regular sessions had finished, enhancing his positional awareness when facing shots or for dominating his area when dealing with crosses, and also refining his saving technique. He had even tweaked the latter while at the England camp in Mexico, staying for extra shot-stopping practice after noticing the rock-hard pitches meant the ball was bouncing higher than back home.

It certainly paid off for what quickly became known as 'the save of the century', although it has remained relevant well into the next one too.

Even now, in an age where goalkeepers' skill with their feet has become as important as how good they are with their hands, it's still the yardstick by which all other amazing stops by any goalkeeper are measured. Take Turkey goalkeeper Mert Günok's wonder-stop against Austria at Euro 2024, for example, which was described by pundits as being a 'Banks replica', 54 years on from the original.

Such heights appeared unlikely at the start of Banks's career. Born in Sheffield in 1937, he was overlooked by the city's two major clubs, Sheffield Wednesday and Sheffield United, and quickly discarded by the Sheffield Schoolboys representative side. When they dropped him, aged 15, his dad insisted he leave school, so he worked as a coalbagger and then apprentice bricklayer on building sites, pausing his football career because he was too tired to play at weekends, before resuming by playing on Sundays for local amateur teams.

A scout from Chesterfield recognised his promise and he joined the Spireites while still a teenager, gaining a first taste of the big time in 1956 when they reached the FA Youth Cup final where they lost to a Manchester United side featuring Bobby Charlton. Then he was posted to Germany on national service and had to wait until he was 21 for his first-team debut in 1958.

He made rapid progress from there and was snapped up by Division One side Leicester City a year later. He was capped twice by England at Under-23 level in 1961 and when Alf Ramsey selected his first England squad, to face France in a European Nations Cup tie on 27 February 1963, Banks was called up at senior level for the first time, as reserve keeper to Ron Springett of Sheffield Wednesday.

At 27, Springett was only 18 months older than Banks, but vastly more experienced at international level having already won 28 caps and played every game at the previous year's World Cup in Chile, when Alan Hodgkinson was back-up and Banks was left at home, on stand-by.

Springett had a nightmare in Paris, however, with his indecision and errors proving costly in a 5–2 defeat and leaving Ramsey looking for a new man to be his last line of defence.

It was Banks who was handed the opportunity but his debut, against Scotland at a revamped Wembley on 6 April, saw more defensive mistakes and a 2–1 defeat to their fierce rivals which made it anything but a dream start.

He kept his spot but did not endear himself to his manager in England's next game, a 1–1 draw with Brazil a month later. Ramsey had warned him to be 'on his toes' if the reigning world champions won a free-kick anywhere near the penalty area and gave Banks what was later described as a 'rollicking' when Pepe bamboozled him before half-time with a bending 'banana' kick that left Banks grasping at thin air as it soared into the net.

A series of second-half saves more than made up for that perceived error, however, and Banks felt he had cemented his new status as England's number one on a summer tour of continental Europe, where he was preferred to Springett in two of the three matches.

That was not the case, however. There was more competition for his position to come from Blackpool's Tony Waiters, who played in five of England's 12 games in 1964, the same year Banks lifted his first trophy at club level – the League Cup with Leicester – and when a minor off-field misdemeanour almost cost him his international place for good.

The England squad had met up in London, a couple of days before flying to Lisbon for an end-of-season friendly with Portugal. Ramsey, a strict disciplinarian, did not allow his players to leave their hotel and certainly did not approve of them enjoying an evening out drinking beer but, when Banks received a knock on his door from captain Bobby Moore and striker Jimmy Greaves, inviting him

Banks tries an American Football kit for size during his time with Fort Lauderdale Strikers in the NASL.

out for what they called 'a quick pint', he was happy to accept.

More future World Cup winners – Bobby Charlton, Ray Wilson and George Eastham, were joined by Johnny Byrne in the small group of seven players that sneaked to a local pub and then extended their evening further at a nearby nightclub. They thought no-one had noticed, until they returned to their rooms in the early hours.

'I immediately knew I was in trouble,' Banks recalled. 'There on my pillow was my passport. Alf's message to me that my place on the plane to Portugal was far from assured. I was still gathering my thoughts when the door opened and in walked the others, all with passports in hand.'

Ramsey did not raise the issue with any of them until just before the Portugal game, but made it clear a repeat would not be tolerated.

'We all knew that our international careers would be finished should we overstep the mark again,' Banks added. 'And even though I played well in Lisbon, where we won 4–3, Alf still dropped me for the next game against the Republic of Ireland.'

Banks would not make the same mistake again. By the time the 1966 World Cup came around, he was established as first-choice for his country. He would go on to play in every minute of their historic triumph at their home tournament.

He did not concede a goal in any of England's group games – a goalless draw against Uruguay and 2–0 victories over Mexico and France – and kept another clean sheet as Argentina were beaten 1–0 in the quarter-finals.

It was the first goal he had conceded in 720 minutes for England . . .

There was some drama before the thrilling semi-final victory over Portugal but only because Banks, who at the time usually played bare-handed rather than using gloves unless the conditions were wet, had forgotten the chewing gum he used to improve his grip on the ball. England coach Harold Shepherdson had to dash down Wembley Way to buy some from a local newsagent while the players were in the tunnel.

Two Bobby Charlton goals put England in control before Portugal fought back with a late penalty, when Eusébio sent Banks the wrong way from the spot. It was the first goal he had conceded in 720 minutes for England, in a record run lasting almost eight games – a milestone that was not bettered until 2021, when Jordan Pickford went 725 minutes without being beaten before Denmark scored early in the semi-final of the European Championship.

Portugal flew forward in search of an equaliser, creating a flurry of chances, and if not for Banks – and a last-minute save that was not quite as spectacular or anywhere near as famous as the one which would deny Pelé, but actually proved to be far more significant – then England's fate could have been very different.

With the final attack of the game, Eusébio made one last run at goal before squaring the ball to find his skipper, Mário Coluna, who found space outside the area to unleash a fierce strike that had Banks, springing to his left, at full stretch to tip the ball over the bar. It's not easy to find on YouTube, but it is his best save of that tournament, and BBC commentator Kenneth Wolstenholme simply calls it 'magnificent'.

Banks did not put a foot wrong in the World Cup final, either. After losing two FA Cup finals at Wembley with Leicester, against Tottenham in 1961 and Manchester United in 1963, he must have feared the worst when Helmut Haller fired West Germany in front after 12 minutes but he was unsighted and could do little about that shot, or Wolfgang Weber's opportunistic close-range strike that took the game to extra-time.

Most of the excitement that followed took place at the other end of the pitch – involving events immortalised by more of

Wolstenholme's words which we will cover elsewhere in this book – but Banks still had work to do to ensure England's triumph.

He expertly dealt with efforts from Haller, Sigfried Held and Uwe Seeler to ensure he would be named goalkeeper of the tournament as well as lift the Jules Rimet Trophy. It took time for his achievement to sink in, but he remembered where it had all started for him as a boy playing park football.

'As I descended the steps from the Royal Box, clutching the medal every player in the world yearns for, I couldn't believe the journey I had made,' he later recalled. 'The road from Tinsley Rec to a World Cup final had been long and winding but the difficulties encountered along the way suddenly evaporated as my whole being was engulfed with euphoria.'

His reliability and consistency coined the phrase 'safe as the Banks of England', a play on a popular saying of the day about the security of the country's primary financial institution, and his talent was recognised globally too. He now held the reputation as being the best in the world at his art – that status being underlined when he won FIFA's

Banks gets his hands on the Jules Rimet Trophy during England's lap of honour at Wembley after the 1966 World Cup final.

Goalkeeper of the Year award every year running between 1966 and 1971.

Domestically, though, he was strangely valued rather less, even in the immediate aftermath of England's triumph. Leicester had a talented teenager by the name of Peter Shilton on their books and decided developing him made more economic sense, so Banks was put up for sale in 1967.

Goalkeepers in this era were criminally undervalued and not deemed worthy of large fees so, while Banks was yet to turn 30, Leicester's asking price of £50,000 was seen as too steep by the leading clubs of the day. Liverpool and West Ham were among those interested but instead he joined the less fashionable Stoke City – a move neither party ended up regretting.

Brazil legend Pelé became close friends with Banks after being denied by his famous save at the 1970 World Cup.

He remained England's mainstay, however, and more trophies with the Three Lions might have followed had Banks not fallen ill with food poisoning a week after that famous save from Pelé in 1970. Although England were beaten 1–0 by Brazil – everyone remembers Banks's save and Pelé's embrace with Bobby Moore at the final whistle, rather than the result – a 1–0 win over Czechoslovakia in their next match had put them into the quarter-finals and a rematch with West Germany, beaten finalists in 1966.

This time, Banks would play no part. Two days before the game, he was permitted a bottle of beer with his evening meal and felt ill soon afterwards. His condition, a combination of fever and stomach cramp, worsened the next day but he felt better on the morning of the match and was able to eat toast for breakfast.

With kick-off at noon to suit European television audiences, he passed what he remembers as being the most gentle of fitness tests on the hotel lawn, but his illness quickly returned and he had to pull out.

Banks's deputy, Peter Bonetti, was a capable keeper but had a terrible day as England saw a 2–0 lead turn into a 3–2 defeat in the sweltering heat, and he has always been blamed for their exit.

That feels harsh in hindsight but Banks was considered the best in the world, so of course he was missed. 'Of all the players we had to lose, we had to lose him,' Ramsey would later lament.

Silverware was proving hard to come by at club level too, as Banks suffered continued frustration in his efforts to win the FA Cup, losing successive semi-finals with Stoke to Arsenal in 1971 and 1972.

Despite being one of the most mild-mannered men in football, Banks was still angry about the manner of those defeats 40 years later, with controversial refereeing decisions costing Stoke each time.

The Gunners went on to lift the FA Cup and clinch the Double in 1971 but Banks was always adamant that the Potters should have progressed instead. They led 2–1 at Hillsborough, deep into stoppage time, when a contentious corner led to a penalty for a John Maloney handball, and a Peter Storey equaliser from the spot.

'Time was up, and I knew if I could deal with an Arsenal free-kick then the game had to be over,' Banks said. 'I came out and got a clean catch, but John Radford hit me in the middle of the back and I couldn't help but drop the ball. It went out for a corner, which of course they scored from. To this day I do not know why the referee did not blow for the foul. It was criminal.

'Of course it still rankles. It would rankle with any footballer to feel that they have been cheated out of reaching a Cup final, and that's exactly what we felt. Not just me, but all the Stoke players.'

Stoke lost the replay, just as they did when the clubs met at the same stage the following season. This time it was an offside decision that went against them, when the linesman had apparently mistaken a steward in a white coat for a Stoke player and allowed Radford to run clear and score, with television footage showing he was a long way offside.

Some consolation, and a long awaited second success at club level, did come Banks's way when he helped Stoke beat Chelsea to win the 1972 League Cup final. Banks's reward was to be named as the Football Writers' Footballer of the Year, the first goalkeeper to win the award since Bert Trautmann in 1956.

He had kept his England place after the 1970 World Cup too, but his 73rd and final appearance came on 27 May 1972 against the team he had faced at the start of his international career. This time, Scotland were beaten 1–0 with Banks keeping a clean sheet.

By now, younger men like Shilton and Liverpool's Ray Clemence were pushing to take his England place but at 34 Banks was still at the top of his game and remained first-choice. Tragically, his opportunity to win more caps was cruelly cut short in October that year.

Banks was driving his Ford Consul home after receiving treatment for a minor injury when he attempted to overtake a car and collided with an Austin A60 coming the other way. He was not wearing a seatbelt – they did not become compulsory in the United Kingdom until 1983 – and when his head went through the windscreen, splinters of glass lodged in his right eye.

He needed 200 stitches to facial injuries and was lucky to be alive, but was told there was only a 50-50 chance that he would see out of that eye again. At first his recovery seemed to be going well, and his vision improved. He even resumed light training with Stoke, while always wearing a patch to guard against infection but, as he described in his autobiography, his hopes were abruptly dashed.

'I was sitting in our living room looking out at the garden when I decided to lift my patch to see whether the improvement was continuing,' Banks wrote. 'I did so and was immediately gripped by fear. Something was very wrong. I closed my left eye and the world went black, I was half blind.

'The surgeon informed me there was nothing more he could do. The edifice of hope I'd erected during the weeks since the crash came tumbling around my ears.'

His career at the highest level was over, although he would return to action in 1977 to play for Fort Lauderdale Strikers in the lucrative but short-lived North American Soccer League, where he was voted Goalkeeper of the Season.

He also spent time in coaching and management with Port Vale and non-league Telford United before the end of that decade. Those were his only spells in the dugout but he was always

As well as 'that' save, Banks made another superb stop to deny Pelé when England met Brazil in Mexico. They would be reunited in the United States at the end of their careers.

involved in the game he loved as a long-term member of the pools panel, who rule on the outcome of postponed matches in England, and was president of Stoke City from 2000 until his death in 2019 at the age of 81.

Pelé led the tributes, reflecting again on the moment that entwined them, and repeated a sentence he had uttered many times down the years when he said: 'I have scored more than a thousand goals in my life and the thing people always talk to me about is the one I didn't score.'

It was always the same for Banks, who realised before he died that no-one would ever forget his most magical moment. 'People still ask me every day about this save,' he posted on social media in 2018. 'It all seems so long ago but that split second kept me remembered seemingly forever.'

Eddie Hapgood captained Arsenal and England and was one of the first footballers to enjoy celebrity status when he became a national hero in the 1930s.

Eddie Hapgood

Born	24 September 1908; died 20 April 1973
Place of birth	Bristol
Position	Defender

Eddie Hapgood played 30 times for England between 1933 and 1939, wearing the captain's armband on 21 occasions. He played in a further 13 wartime internationals during World War II and was skipper in all those games.

Eddie Hapgood made the fewest England appearances of any player to make it into this book, and he is also the only man on my list of Immortals whose career came before the Second World War, or indeed the 1966 World Cup.

His era was very different to those that followed but still significant, not just because it saw the start of the huge changes in the landscape of international football that would affect England's standing globally, but because of the volatile political situation in Europe that framed them.

In the absence of a manager – England did not get one of those until Walter Winterbottom was appointed in 1946 – Hapgood's role as captain was very different from those that followed him, and none of them led their teams into quite the type of arenas that he did. He did so with such distinction it is surprising that he is often overlooked in any discussion of all-time greats.

But, before we start exploring his part in England's past and how some of his experiences read like a real life version of Michael Caine's character Captain John Colby in the cult classic football film *Escape to Victory*, I should explain there is a reason why this team is mostly made up of players from the last 50 years in England's history, rather than the first 90 or so.

Not only did England refuse to enter formal global or continental competition until the 1950 World Cup, they also played mostly British or Irish sides in those early years. Of their 163 international matches between 1872 and the beginning of 1929, only 22 were against foreign opposition, which I will define here as teams other than Scotland, Wales, Ireland or Northern Ireland.

There was a higher turnover of England players then, too, as well as fewer games and Hapgood was only the second man to wear the white shirt on 30 or more occasions, after Bob Crompton of Blackburn Rovers, who played 41 times between 1902 and 1914 and was the first fully professional footballer to captain his country. All of this meant they had fewer opportunities to play in meaningful matches, other than in the Home Championship, or become household names.

Hapgood, here holding the base of the trophy, celebrates after helping Arsenal win the 1936 FA Cup. He won five League titles with the Gunners, and two FA Cups.

Hapgood achieved both, and became a national hero, despite being something of a late-starter football-wise. When he left school at 14 in 1922, he did not have a team and had never even played in an organised game. Instead, he began his working life in his home city of Bristol at the Great Western Cotton Works, where he lasted less than a week before being fired for asking for higher wages, before joining the dairy business run by his sister's husband, Jack Sibley.

Playing for his country was probably never in his thoughts. Back then, the route into football was very different from the one taken by aspiring England players of today, who are often identified as future stars before they reach double digits, nurtured in clubs' academies where they are given years of top-class coaching, and paid mind-boggling sums when they have barely become young adults.

In contrast, Hapgood only played his first official 11-a-side match at the age of 17, when he swapped playing games in the street with his friends for wearing the colours of St Philip's Marsh Adult School F.C. who, as their name suggests, were a senior club – but one that also entered youth teams in the Bristol Downs League on Saturdays.

He continued working full-time as a milkman, but his performances in his first season as an elegant and exceptionally calm left-back began to attract the attention of scouts on the lookout for young talent. In May 1927, he was invited to sign a professional contract by Bristol Rovers, one of the city's two Football League clubs. Hapgood had impressed on trial but rejected Rovers because the club's offer of supplementary employment during the summer meant he would be driving a coal cart, which he viewed as a step down from delivering milk.

It seems an odd decision now, but when you learn more about Hapgood's early days, the single-mindedness he shows when leading England later in his life shines through, and so does the sense of justice and desire for a 'fair deal' that his daughter Lynne describes so eloquently in the biography *Footballer From Beyond The Touchline* that she wrote about her father in 2022.

If Hapgood felt he deserved better than a coal cart, then he was quickly proved right. While the first move he ended up making that summer – to non-league side Kettering Town – represented modest progress, by October of that year, when he had just turned 19 and had played only nine first-team games for his new club, he was heading straight to the First Division with Herbert Chapman's Arsenal, a hugely ambitious club who at that time had not won a single major trophy in the first 45 years of their existence, but were about to make up for that lack of silverware in spectacular style.

He was now in the big time, but his motivation to improve did not stop there. Like Gordon Banks, and so many other England greats, Hapgood was committed to making the most of his abilities and spent many extra hours training alone, in his case enhancing his strength and physical capabilities as well as his skills. Indeed, his attitude had already impressed Chapman before he signed him because, unlike many of his contemporaries, Hapgood did not drink or smoke.

Hapgood would go on to captain Arsenal, with whom he won an incredible five league titles over the next 11 years, but he had to wait to establish himself at Highbury, and also for his chance at international level – although the latter was partly his own decision. The first time he was selected by England, in May 1930 when he was chosen for their summer tour of Europe, he decided not to travel because his wife Maggie was due to give birth to their first child, Anthony.

How much that decision annoyed the national team's selection committee is unclear. England's regular left-back, Sheffield Wednesday's Ernest Blenkinsop was highly regarded so it was not simply a case of Hapgood being deliberately snubbed, but it was still almost three years later, with Arsenal by now the dominant force in English club football, before his country belatedly came calling again, for another summer tour of Europe.

This time Hapgood would make his debut, at the age of 24, against Italy in Rome in May 1933. It was certainly eventful, even if the tale he tells in his 1945 autobiography *Football Ambassador* of how a wayward clearance found a notorious target seems unlikely to be completely true.

If Hapgood felt he deserved better than a coal cart, then he was quickly proved right.

One of the spectators at a packed Stadio del Partito Nazionale Fascista was Italian dictator Benito Mussolini, who was aware of the important part that football success could play in propaganda purposes for his country. Italy were preparing to host the 1934 World Cup and Mussolini's plan was to win it, but first he wanted to topple England, who were viewed as the 'old masters' and would represent quite a scalp.

What Mussolini did not see coming, apparently, was the ball when Hapgood fired it into the crowd to stop an early Italy attack. 'It crashed against his tightly fitting uniform, just above his lunch' is how Hapgood describes the incident although it seems he was told what happened by one of the England party nearby rather than witnessing it himself.

Understandably, Hapgood still enjoyed telling the tale, and his subsequent notoriety, adding how 'my friend told me "Musso", when he got his breath back, looked

Hapgood was Arsenal's skipper during a decade when they enjoyed unprecedented success.

like he wanted to kill the man who had outraged his dignity.'

Whether that story is embellished or not, Hapgood made an impression on the pitch too. The final score was 1–1 and, in his report for the *News Chronicle*, prominent football reporter of the day Charles Buchan described England's 'gallant defenders' and included Hapgood on a list of five men who 'played the game of their lives'.

It was quite a way to start any England career but still had nothing on Hapgood's first game as captain of his country 18 months later in November 1934, again against Italy, which goes down as one of the most brutal encounters in the long history of the Three Lions.

Hapgood, who with a badly broken nose was among the many casualties, describes it as 'the dirtiest match I have ever played in' and it is known as the 'Battle of Highbury' for good reason, but in the build-up it had been billed as the true World Championship match. Italy had indeed won the World Cup earlier that year but, while England had declined to enter, they had never been beaten at home by a non-British or Irish team, and still saw themselves as the true footballing force on the planet as well as the pioneers of the sport.

Wartime internationals attracted huge crowds, with gate receipts donated to the Red Cross. Here, Prime Minister Winston Churchill is introduced to the England team by Hapgood before a game against Scotland at Wembley in October 1941.

They ended up preserving that proud unbeaten record, but this win was one that literally came after one heck of a fight. There have been many England matches down the years that, for various reasons, have turned into battles which invoked analogies of actual conflict, but this was the first time it had happened on such a scale and it brought an alarmed reaction from the media. Hapgood remembered how one journalist signed off his report as being 'by our war correspondent', and the events clearly rattled the Football Association, who considered banning all international games in the aftermath.

It did not take long for a bruising and bloody encounter to take shape. Hapgood was of seven Arsenal players in the England XI who were playing on home ground, and one of his club-mates, Ted Drake, landed the first of many blows after only two minutes when his challenge broke the ankle of Italy's Argentina-born defender Luis Monti and, in the days before substitutes, reduced them to 10 men.

The rest of the Italy team felt Drake had deliberately hurt Monti and set about getting their revenge, with outraged newspaper accounts of the time describing them as attacking England players at the same time their hosts were building a healthy early advantage.

Eric Brook had already missed a penalty when Monti was injured, but made amends with two goals before Hapgood was hurt, in what in his eyes was far from an accident.

'The ball went into touch on my side of the field and, to save time, the Italian right winger threw the ball in,' he recalled. 'It went high over me and, as I doubled back to collar it, the right-half, without making any effort whatsoever to get the ball, jumped up in front of me and carefully smashed his elbow into my face.'

Hapgood, who was briefly left unconscious, was carried off and was in the dressing room getting rudimentary treatment on his nose – 'felt supports on either side and strapping plaster on' – when Drake put England 3–0 ahead, all inside the first 15 minutes, but soon 'jumped up and ran out on to the field again' to help hold off a determined Italy fightback in the second half.

The final score was 3–2 but the goals were outnumbered by injuries. As well as Hapgood, Drake was sporting two black eyes and 'legs torn to ribbons' according to *The Guardian's* correspondent at the game, with John Barker (lost tooth, cut eye and left hand bandaged), Ray Bowden (ankle), Brook (X-ray on his arm) and Wilf Copping (bandaged left leg) all needing treatment.

Even then, the hostilities were not finished. At the post-match banquet that evening, Hapgood described how 'the England team looked a sorry sight', including himself. As he made his way to the front of the room, nose still in plaster, he passed his assailant from that afternoon.

'He looked me straight in the eyes . . . and laughed,' Hapgood wrote. 'I'm glad I'm a pretty even-tempered fellow or I would have gone across the table at him, but he wasn't worth it.'

That was not the only time where Hapgood had to display skills of diplomacy that matched his artful and assured style of defending, but it was a rare occasion where he was given a choice of how to react.

He was seen as one of the heroes of the day and his bravery

in returning to the game, with his white shirt covered in blood, as well as his fairness when he did re-appear on the pitch, only enhanced his growing reputation nationally – he was not just an England player now, he was their recognised leader.

Hapgood would keep the captain's armband for the remainder of his international career but, while it brought the reward of added fame and, with it, the welcome extra income of some early endorsement deals – including one for Mars Bars – this was a time when there was next to no 'player power', so it did not give him any influence about who England might play, or alter how he and his team were told they should behave.

Two politically charged games with Germany, almost three years apart, demonstrated that. The first was at Tottenham's White Hart Lane ground in December 1935, a friendly supposedly designed to demonstrate the strong relations between the two nations. It went ahead, despite protests by anti-fascist groups and Jewish communities, with England – who were supposedly 'playing for international peace' – winning 3–0.

By the time England went to Berlin in May 1938, Europe was even more on edge. At that point, the British government's approach to the Nazi Germany regime was one of appeasement, including at sporting fixtures, which meant the team were expected to give the Nazi salute during the German anthem before kick-off. Hapgood later called it 'the worst moment of my life' and it remains one of the most controversial incidents in British sporting history.

There are conflicting accounts of how the final decision about giving the salute was made, exactly who ordered it to happen and also who was against it but, seeing as it went ahead, it is clear any protests the players did make were ignored. As captain, Hapgood remembered being instructed on the eve of the game by Football Association secretary Stanley Rous and tour manager Charles Wreford-Brown, who were under guidance of the British ambassador to Germany, Sir Nevile Henderson.

Hapgood wrote: 'I replied, "we are of the British Empire and I do not see any reason why we should give the Nazi salute; they should understand that we always stand to attention for every National Anthem. We have never done it before – we have always stood to attention, but we will do everything we can to beat them fairly and squarely." I then went out to see the rest of the lads to tell them what was in the offing. There was much muttering in the ranks.'

When those objections were raised again by Hapgood and other members of the team in the changing room just before the game, Rous and Wreford-Brown explained the seriousness of the situation and, according to another England player, Stanley Matthews, they told the players that a failure to salute could be 'the spark that set Europe alight'.

As captain, Hapgood clearly felt he had no choice but to comply. 'That was that, and we were all pretty miserable about it,' he recalled. 'Personally, I felt a fool Heiling Hitler, but Mr Rous's diplomacy worked, for we went out determined to beat the Germans.'

Adolf Hitler was not at the game but Rudolph Hess, Hermann Göring and Joseph Goebbels were among the prominent Nazis who were present. Although it received relatively little media criticism at the time and none of that was attributed to the players, the image of the England football team saluting them is seen now as shameful and an endorsement

. . . he was not just an England player now, he was their recognised leader.

Hapgood hits the golf course with fellow England star Stanley Matthews. Unlike Hapgood, Matthews resumed his top-level career after the war ended.

of their politics. In 2003, the BBC said it 'ranks as one of England's darkest moments in the sport'.

The game that followed was 'something of a footnote' according to Ulrich Linder, co-author of *Strikers for Hitler*, a 1999 book which examines German football between 1933 and 1945. It's true that the significance of the day in England's football history has nothing to do with the final score, but to Hapgood and his team-mates, their performance and the result was all-important.

They played brilliantly to win 6–3 in front of a crowd of more than 100,000 and Hapgood's pride in his team's display was evident when he wrote about it a few years later, calling it 'perhaps one of the greatest wins of all time by an English soccer side' and 'certainly the most satisfactory', even if by then he realised the extent that he and his team-mates had been exploited.

If Berlin saw Hapgood's worst moment with England, it was not long before Hampden Park would provide his best. In April 1939, he led England to their first win in Scotland for 12 years, and again demonstrated why he was appointed as the team's figurehead.

'Going up in the train I used all my eloquence on the rest of the team and told them the Scots weren't supermen, that 11 Englishmen were as good as 11 Scots any day, and other things to the same effect,' Hapgood remembered. 'In the hotel I continued my pep talk, and carried on in the dressing room until I must have hypnotised the team into thinking the match was as good as won.'

His recollection is not overblown. Stanley Matthews, who played in this game too, would later describe how inspirational his captain's pep talk was, saying: 'It was obvious Eddie had made up his mind we weren't going to lose and when Eddie was in that sort of mood, it was infectious.'

It worked. In front of a crowd of 149,269, and in rain so heavy that a soaked England team were forced to change into the kit of local club Queens Park at half-time, Tommy Lawton's late goal gave England a 2–1 win that had Hapgood dancing a jig of delight.

'I have realised my last ambition,' he told reporters after the game and, when he wrote about it later, the chapter on this game was titled 'My Greatest Match'.

Another tour of Europe followed soon afterwards, departing for Milan on the Orient Express in May, but it would be the last time

Hapgood was rewarded for his role as England captain during the Second World War with a meeting with King George VI.

Hapgood would represent his country overseas. The trip took in Italy, where he met Mussolini again, and Yugoslavia, where he suffered an ankle injury after 15 minutes but, typically, finished the game.

He had damaged ligaments and was ruled out of the final game of the tour, in Romania, which would also mark the end of full internationals for England for more than eight years.

When war broke out in September 1939, it finished Hapgood's professional career too. Like every other player, his club contract was torn up and he had to find work elsewhere – in his case, with the Police Reserve Unit – before he was called up to serve as physical training instructor with the RAF.

Football continued, however, and for Hapgood that included friendly club games – mostly for Arsenal, but also including guest appearances for teams near where he was stationed – plus representative games for the Armed Forces and also wartime internationals. England played 36 of

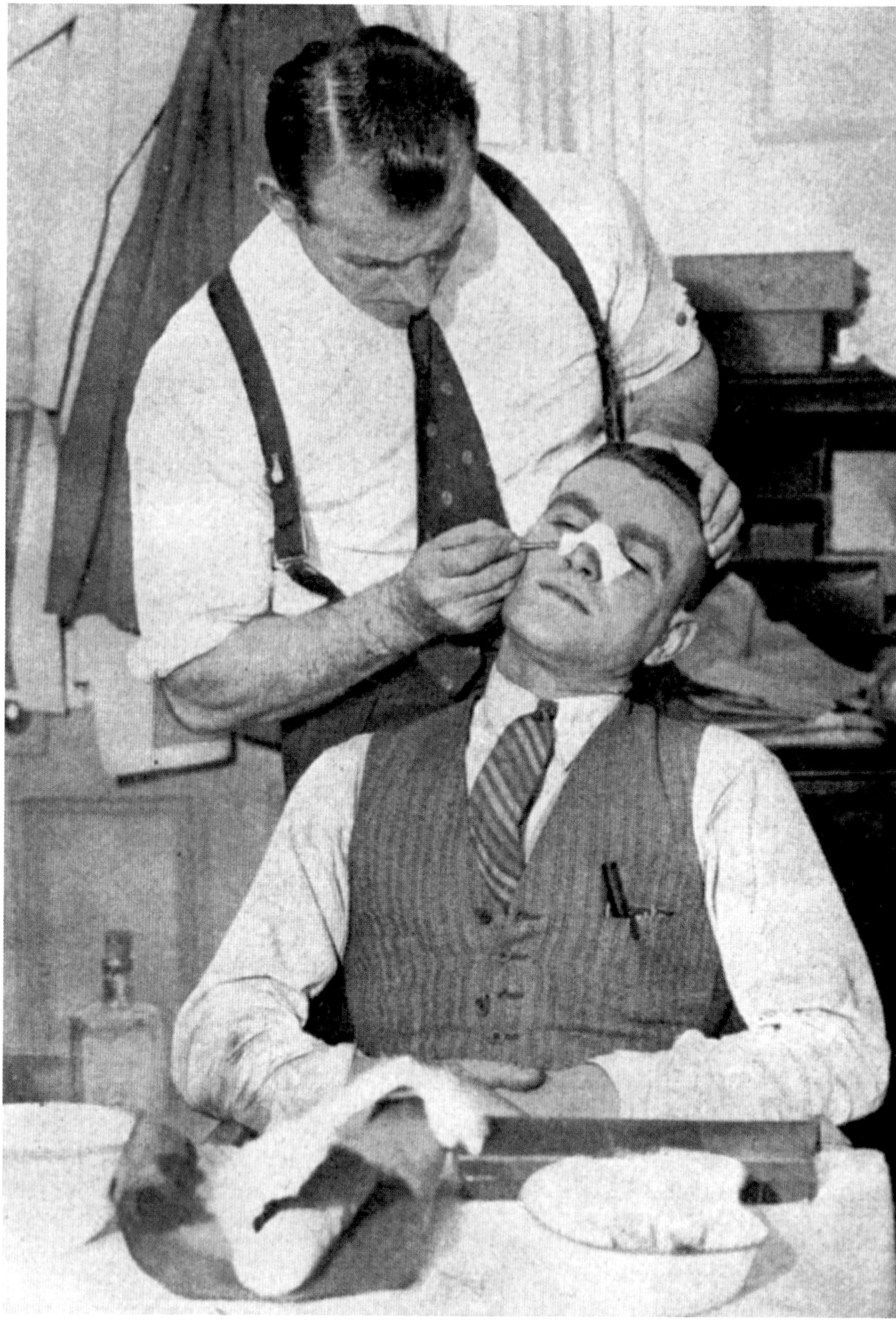

Hapgood is treated for the broken nose he sustained in the 'Battle of Highbury'.

those in total, with Hapgood involved in 13 of them between 1939 and 1943.

These games must have brought some escape from the reality of war, for players and spectators alike, but its shadow was never far away. In 1940, when Hapgood captained the England side that travelled to Glasgow to take on Scotland, a crowd of 61,000 came to watch but 9,000 ticket-holders stayed away because of a transmission from Nazi propaganda broadcaster Lord Haw-Haw before the game stating that the Luftwaffe would flatten Hampden Park by half-time.

Hapgood covers this period in his book, which is the earliest example of a footballer's autobiography, detailing visits to 'bomb-scarred' grounds like St Andrews, home of Birmingham City, and it is almost completely devoid of the joy with which he recounted his earlier adventures abroad with England.

There was one last highlight, however, that saw his England career given the send-off it deserved before his final appearance for his country, against Wales at Wembley in February 1943.

The FA announced they were to honour Hapgood's role during the war by including his 12 previous wartime games in his official tally, which meant he had broken Crompton's record of 41 appearances, with 22 as captain. His reward included a meeting with King George VI after the game, which England won 5–3.

There was one last highlight, however, that saw his England career given the send-off it deserved . . .

Sadly his club, Arsenal, did not treat him so well when the war ended and competitive club football resumed in 1946, when he was 37. Hapgood expected a long-service bonus but the Gunners refused, saying the games he played during the war years did not count, and they would not award him a testimonial either.

After retiring, he had spells in charge of Blackburn, Watford and Bath City but left football in 1956 to run YMCA hostels. He died on Good Friday 1973, aged 64.

One of the most iconic images in British sporting history. Bobby Moore sitting on his team-mates' shoulders at Wembley, holding aloft the Jules Rimet Trophy.

Bobby Moore

Born	12 April 1941; died 24 February 1993
Place of birth	Barking, Essex
Position	Defender

Bobby Moore played 108 times for his country between May 1962 and November 1973 and wore the armband on 90 occasions, equalling Billy Wright's record for games as skipper. Moore's England World Cup winning manager Sir Alf Ramsey called him 'my captain, my leader, my right-hand man', while Pelé said 'of all the defenders I have challenged, Bobby Moore was the fairest, the best and the most honourable'.

It is hard enough to select just 11 of England's legends let alone single one of them out, but there are several reasons why Bobby Moore can be considered England's greatest ever player and it does not rely on the fact he is their only captain to win the World Cup.

His long-time manager at West Ham, Ron Greenwood, once told *The Guardian* newspaper that 'Bobby is not a bread-and-butter player, he is made for the biggest occasions. The more extreme the challenge, the more commanding he will be. He should play at Wembley every week.'

For a spell, it felt like that almost was the case. Moore's early successes as Hammers skipper – an FA Cup triumph in 1964 followed by victory in the European Cup Winners' Cup final in 1965 – both took place underneath the old national stadium's Twin Towers and he would return there to complete a unique hat-trick in 1966, carefully wiping his hands clean on his shirt, shorts and the black velvet that lined the Royal Box before

Another Wembley win. Moore kisses the FA Cup after West Ham's victory in the 1964 final.

shaking the Queen's hand, so as not to get sweat on her white gloves before she presented him with the most celebrated trophy of all.

Moore's magic was multi-faceted, and I will try to do justice to each aspect here, but some of it can be easily seen in the poise, composure and character that are captured forever in the images that define him.

The best known, of course, is the iconic photo of him on the shoulders of his team-mates at Wembley, holding the Jules Rimet Trophy aloft in English football's finest hour, but there is also the TV footage of his perfectly timed tackle on Brazilian great Jairzinho at the 1970 World Cup and his embrace with Pelé when they exchanged shirts at the end of that game.

That was the sort of spirit and style which was evident throughout Moore's career as a natural leader at centre-half, which saw him become famous as a player able to quickly sense and skilfully avert danger, as well as for the coolness under pressure that he personified.

Off the pitch, he dealt with everything he faced without a fuss too, from his battle with life-threatening testicular cancer only 18 months before helping England become world champions in 1966, to being wrongly accused of theft while in Colombia before the 1970 tournament.

Part of his unflappable nature can surely be traced back to his upbringing. Moore was born in London's East End at the very height of the Blitz and had to be evacuated from his home in Barking when he was just a few hours old because German bombs hit houses up his street.

'I don't think anyone is not aware of the strength of character of the British people under the German bombing,' Moore's biographer and close friend Jeff Powell told a BBC TV documentary in 2006. 'Bobby's parents were of the generation of people who held firm and Bobby grew up with that mentality – that nothing could not be overcome, basically.'

It was that mindset that would see him conquer the flaws in his game and rise through the ranks for club and country after joining his local side West Ham as an apprentice at the age of 15.

Given how he is remembered, it may be surprising to learn that Moore was not always seen as a superstar in the making, but he was no childhood footballing prodigy. His boyhood nickname was 'Tubby', and he was often the last to be picked when teams were selected for the games he played in Barking Park with his friends.

Like so many other players mentioned in this book, however, Moore always had the inner drive to make the most of his talent, starting with the hours of practice he put in when he decided at a young age that he had to improve his weaker left foot. He retained that work ethic when he got older, and it helped him become one of the finest ball-playing defenders in history.

West Ham scout Wally St Pier saw some of that potential when he spotted him playing in Dagenham aged 14 and, according to Powell, declared 'here is a boy who is going to play for England', but the club's coaching staff were not as convinced. Moore was also the 'last pick' for the Hammers, who only chose him in the 13th and final slot they had for new apprentices on their intake of groundstaff in 1956.

Initially, his future international team-mate Geoff Hurst was not particularly impressed by Moore's ability either, although his other qualities did stand out when they lined up together as teenagers for the Hammers youth team.

Hurst joined West Ham shortly after Moore and wrote in 2014 that 'when we first played together he was fairly green and certainly wasn't one of the outstanding players at the club', but then describes his old friend as having an 'obsession for perfection'.

He remembered one particular pre-season drill to develop core strength where players would lie on their backs and the last man to allow his feet to touch the ground would win a prize. Even as an apprentice, Moore would not be outdone by the club's senior professionals.

'Even in training he had to win,' Hurst explained. 'The sort of attitude that managers dream of seeing in their players.' It was that kind of determination that quickly took him to the highest echelons of the game, allied by another key quality Moore possessed – his intelligence on the field.

'St Pier said Bobby was head and shoulders above anything else he had ever seen,' Powell told the BBC's *Captain Fantastic* documentary in 2002. 'He was also the first to say that Bobby's attributes were difficult to recognise because he appeared to be limited in many areas, but the way he compensated indicated even at that age a great football brain, and Bobby's game was based on intelligence.'

His speed of thought made up for a relative lack of pace and limited heading ability, and meant his weaknesses were rarely exposed as he rapidly rose through the ranks. In 1964, the same year he helped West Ham beat Preston North End 3–2 to lift the FA Cup for the first time, he became the youngest ever Footballer of the Year.

Moore was destined for even greater things, but not before he had survived a serious illness that he kept secret from even his closest colleagues and friends.

At first, it was thought he was suffering testicular pain because of a sporting injury but his condition continued to worsen, and cancer was quickly diagnosed when he went to see the family GP.

He underwent an orchidectomy for the removal of one of his testicles in November 1964, but this was not made public at the time and his absence from the team was explained by a groin injury.

Three months later he was back in action, but not without some psychological scars. His first wife Tina described how Moore suffered from insomnia during his recovery but never spoke about his diagnosis or treatment or revealed his mental struggles. 'On the surface, you would never know,' she told the BBC in 2010.

His playing performances were certainly not affected. In May 1965 he was back at Wembley with West Ham and starred against German side 1860 Munich as his side won 2–0 to secure their first European trophy.

When another of his old England team-mates, Jimmy Greaves, helped put together a selection of the greatest games he had seen for a 1989 book, he included that Hammers performance in his list.

'West Ham produced one of the finest footballing displays ever seen at Wembley, and a lot of the credit must go to Munich for matching West Ham's spirit of adventure,' Greaves wrote. '"Mooro" was his usual reliable and ice-cool self. England have not had a finer servant. He was an immaculate defender, stamping his authority on every match, and he read the game better than any other player.'

Greenwood hailed that performance as Moore's best yet and described it as 'technical

'Even in training he had to win. The sort of attitude that managers dream of in their players.'
– *Geoff Hurst*

Pelé and Moore's mutual admiration was evident when they embraced after Brazil beat England at the 1970 World Cup.

perfection', but his career had not yet reached its pinnacle – that would come with his country.

Moore's story at international level had started as a teenager with a record 18 games for England's youth team and he made another eight appearances for the Under-23s before an ankle injury to future Three Lions manager Bobby Robson on the eve of the 1962 World Cup opened the door for him to make his full international debut at the age of 21 in a 4–0 friendly win against Peru in Lima on 20 May 1962.

'We all knew that Bobby had potential,' Robson told *FourFourTwo* magazine in 2003. 'He was a good-looking boy with all that blonde hair and had something about him. He came in and just grew and grew as a player, and what a player. If you are going to lose your place to anybody, why not Bobby Moore?'

Bizarrely, Pelé and Moore would later became team-mates when they played in the North American Soccer League in the 1970s. They were both picked to play for Team America in a four-team international tournament to mark the 200th birthday of the United States, playing against Brazil, England and Italy.

Moore did so well that he stayed in the team for the whole tournament, excelling as he helped Walter Winterbottom's side reach the quarter-finals where they lost to holders and eventual winners Brazil. Less than a year later he marked his 12th full cap by captaining his country for the first time in a 4–2 win over Czechoslovakia in Bratislava, becoming the youngest man to lead England at the age of 22 years and 47 days – a record that still stands.

By the summer of 1966, Moore was the first name on Ramsey's team-sheet, and he would play in every game of England's World Cup triumph on home soil – although a contract issue with West Ham almost kept him out of the tournament which would define him.

Tottenham had made an offer for Moore, whose deal expired at the end of the 1965–66 season, but Greenwood told him he was not prepared to let him leave. Moore wanted the move, for a new challenge and higher wages, and the stand-off continued as the start of the World Cup loomed with manager and player trading blows about the situation via the press.

By then Moore was a free agent, and FIFA regulations stated that, because he was not registered with a club and therefore affiliated with the English Football Association, he was not eligible to take part. It took an intervention from Ramsey on 9 July, just two days before the opening game, to end the stand-off. Greenwood was summoned to the England team hotel in Hendon, and the pair were given a short deadline to sort their differences out. It worked, and England had their captain back.

With Moore at the heart of their defence, alongside a more rugged stopper in the shape of Jack Charlton, England did not concede a goal in the group stage and, after drawing with Uruguay in their first match, easily beat Mexico and France to finish top of Group One.

An altogether tougher test awaited them in the quarter-finals and all of Moore's leadership qualities were needed to calmly guide his side through an infamous battle against Argentina, who kicked, spat, pinched and punched the England team through a match which provided one of the most controversial moments in World Cup history when the South American champions' skipper Antonio Rattin refused to leave the field after being shown a red card in the first half.

It was down to Moore to ensure that England kept their heads and held their nerve . . .

German referee Rudolf Kreitlein had dismissed Rattin for his bad language while protesting a decision but Rattin took 10 minutes to depart, demanding a translator and claiming the dismissal was unfair. It was down to Moore to ensure England kept their heads and held their nerve against opposition that Ramsey would later call 'animals'.

'We didn't have a problem, Argentina had the problem,' Jack's brother Bobby Charlton told the BBC in 2001. 'They had created this mayhem. We didn't know how far you could go with the referee. You know there is a limit but they seemed to go well beyond the limit.

'Bobby would be telling everyone that although all this mayhem is going on at the moment and we can't really say what is going to happen, we have to make sure that it doesn't affect us because that's maybe one of the reasons why they are perpetrating the thing in the first place.

'We had to keep our concentration, we had to make sure we had our balance and it didn't influence any change in our marking, and that's what he would be talking about.'

Moore became renowned for his elegant style of play and composure on the pitch.

They got the job done, with a late Geoff Hurst goal giving them a 1–0 win. Next came another defensive masterclass in a 2–1 semi-final victory over a free-scoring Portugal side, who were kept in check until Eusébio's late penalty – the first goal England had conceded in the tournament.

And so to the final. Moore was known as being the man for the big occasion, and so it proved in front of what is still the biggest TV audience in British history, of 32.3 million viewers.

West Germany stunned the Wembley crowd and everyone else who was watching when they took an early lead but Moore's first significant contribution of the day arrived soon afterwards, when his quick thinking was behind England's equaliser.

Moore, always attack-minded whoever the opposition and no matter the occasion, had embarked on a run up the left flank and won a free-kick midway into the West Germany half when he was fouled by Wolfgang Overath. Instead of delaying the set-piece to allow the likes of Jack Charlton to get forward, Moore instantly looked to take it himself, and his precise lofted pass found Hurst bursting into space in the penalty area to nod England level.

'The one thing about the final that I'll remember is how quick Bobby was when he was fouled, and immediately popped the ball down to Geoff, knowing exactly where Geoff would be,' Bobby Charlton told the BBC when asked to talk about Moore's contribution to the final.

As history tells us, there was more to come from England, and Moore. The whole team were heroes but, without his trademark coolness at the end of extra-time, there would be no Hurst hat-trick and no 4–2 scoreline.

With seconds to go, England are 3–2 up and hanging on. But when Banks punches a corner away the ball falls to Moore inside his own penalty area and, rather than smashing it into Row Z, as his team-mates and most of the crowd implore, he elects to chest it down, exchange passes with Roger Hunt and then dribble forwards.

Bobby Charlton added: 'Anyone that watches the last minutes of the extra time will remember everybody is shouting "kick the ball out, kick it out . . . get the ball out of trouble."

'Instead he stopped, he pulled it to his left foot, he pulled it to his right foot. He had a look up, he waited for a little while and then he just released the ball right at the time, over the top of the defence . . .'

The pass is perfectly weighted for a galloping Hurst to wallop his shot into the top corner and secure England's triumph. The celebrations could begin and Moore would soon have his hands on the Jules Rimet Trophy. As commentator Kenneth Wolstenholme so eloquently put it: 'It's only 12 inches tall, solid gold, and it means England are world champions.'

If everything went according to plan in 1966, you could argue the opposite applied for England's defence of their trophy four years later. Their problems started before the tournament had even begun and Moore, who had retained the captaincy, was a global sensation again – but this time for all the wrong reasons.

He was detained in Colombia, where England had played a friendly to acclimatise to the heat and altitude they would face in Mexico, after being arrested and charged with the theft of a gold bracelet from a shop in the foyer of the team hotel.

While the rest of the England squad proceeded to their tournament base, Moore was kept under house arrest for four days, before being allowed to join his team-mates in Leon after the personal intervention of British prime minister Harold Wilson.

The flimsy case against Moore was never properly followed up but it was still the worst possible preparation for a World Cup. He lost a significant amount of weight during his detention and then again following his first training session back with the squad, but typically he did not let his annoyance affect him, no matter how much he felt aggrieved.

The incident would not define his World Cup, either. Instead we have the memories of his high-risk but stunningly precise challenge on Jairzinho as the Brazilian burst into the England penalty area and then that moment of mutual respect with Pelé when, both bare-chested, they smile and congratulate each other at the final whistle of a match of the very highest calibre.

It was only a group game, and one that England lost 1–0, but it was a rare meeting of two superstars – Pelé and Moore only faced each other three times at international level, and this was their sole competitive clash – and remains an illustration of supreme sportsmanship at the highest level. They became lifelong friends.

England still made it through to the quarter-finals despite that defeat but a famous fightback by West Germany meant their

Moore wiped his hands before shaking the Queen's hand after the 1966 World Cup final, so as not to get her white gloves dirty.

journey ended there, with a 3–2 defeat. It would prove to be Moore's last game at a World Cup finals and marked the end of England's glory days – they would not be back at a major tournament for another 12 years.

Moore briefly lost his England place at the start of 1971 as part of the punishment he faced for his involvement in a drinking session before West Ham's FA Cup tie in Blackpool. Thinking the game would be postponed because the pitch at Bloomfield Road was frozen, Moore and a few team-mates headed out and ended up a few hours later at boxer Brian London's nightclub.

The next day, the game went ahead and the Hammers lost 4–0. A story leaked out that Moore had been drinking heavily while out on the town – although he always denied it – and he was fined by West Ham and then dropped by Ramsey for a game in Malta.

He quickly returned to Ramsey's team and remained a commanding and reassuring presence but the few errors he made would prove costly.

Moore was at fault when England bowed out of the European Championship in 1972, again at the quarter-final stage, and again against West Germany.

The damage was done in the first leg at Wembley, beginning when he attempted to dribble out of his area in the same way he had done so successfully at the same venue in 1966 but was caught in possession by Uli Hoeness, who fired past Banks.

The Bobby Moore statue at Wembley.

Francis Lee equalised but, with six minutes to go, Moore made another uncharacteristic mistake when he brought down Sigfried Held inside the area after being outsprinted down the left. Günter Netzer converted from the spot before Gerd Müller added a third goal to leave England with an unsurmountable task in the second leg.

It was a similar story in Moore's final competitive outing for England, a vital World Cup qualifier against Poland in Chorzow in June 1973. He played an unfortunate part in Poland's first goal, when he deflected Robert Gadocha's free-kick past Gordon Banks at his near post, and then was caught in possession by Wlodek Lubański, who ran clear to seal a 2–0 win.

Moore broke Bobby Charlton's England appearance record with his 107th cap against Italy a few days later but missed the return against Poland at Wembley four months later, when a 1–1 draw ensured England were eliminated. His 108th and final

> At 33, his international career was over, but at club level he would manage one last hurrah . . .

appearance for his country came in November when Italy clinched a 1–0 friendly win.

At 33, his international career was over, but at club level he would manage one last hurrah when he helped Second Division side Fulham reach the FA Cup final in 1975. His former club West Ham were the opposition for what proved to be Moore's 47th and last appearance at Wembley but there was no fairytale farewell for him – the Hammers won 2–0.

Sadly, his status and celebrity did not bring him many opportunities in the game he loved when his playing days in England ended in 1977 at the age of 36, after 19 years and 1,000 senior games. He wanted to go into management but a lack of offers meant he returned to the pitch, playing in the United States and Denmark, and featuring as a wartime footballer in the film *Escape to Victory*.

He did have spells in the dugout during the early 1980s in charge of non-league Oxford City, Eastern Athletic in Hong Kong and Division Three side Southend United but ultimately all proved unsuccessful.

Moore moved into the media, becoming sports editor of tabloid *Sunday Sport* in 1986 and then becoming a radio co-commentator and analyst with London station Capital Gold in 1989, where he worked until his death from bowel cancer in 1993, aged 51.

His life is commemorated by a statue outside the new Wembley Stadium, looking out on Wembley Way. The tribute was commissioned by the Football Association, who had held a poll in 2005 to determine England's greatest player of the previous 50 years. Moore was the overwhelming winner.

Stuart Pearce epitomises the determination and desire shown by all of England's greatest players with his passion and will to win.

4

STUART PEARCE

Born	24 April 1962
Place of birth	Shepherd's Bush, London
Position	Defender

Stuart Pearce played 78 games for England between 1987 and 1999, losing only eight times. He scored five goals for his country and captained them on 10 occasions. He started his career at non-league Wealdstone and went on to play for five professional clubs but is best known for a 12-year stint at Nottingham Forest, where he won the League Cup twice.

Stuart Pearce has kicked a football millions of times in his life, in the park and on the pitch, in his back garden and in some of the biggest games possible, but it's just two of those kicks, six years apart, that he is best known for.

When you put it like that, it sounds ridiculous that his career, let alone his character, could be captured by those kicks and their consequences, but the reason they resonate for how we remember Pearce the person as well as Pearce the player is that they were both penalties, both in shootouts at major tournaments for England and, crucially, while the first was a failure, the second was successful.

Shootouts, and specifically the fear of them, have had a unique hold on the psyche of English football fans for decades, so perhaps that is why a man nicknamed 'Psycho' has a special place in their hearts for refusing to hide from such an extreme emotional experience. Instead he repeated it to complete his recovery – and showed how much it meant with the cathartic celebration that followed.

As Pearce says in his 2020 autobiography, 'I wasn't actively seeking redemption for missing the critical penalty in the shootout at the end of the 1990 World Cup semi-final against West Germany, but redemption found me anyway. It found me at the end of the Euro '96 quarter-final against Spain, when there was another penalty shootout and I took another penalty.'

Pearce scored that one, of course, but we should probably start with the miss – or to be more accurate, Bodo Illgner's save – at Stadio Delle Alpi on 4 July 1990.

For context, although at the time this was the furthest England had ever gone in a tournament on foreign shores, it was also their first penalty shootout anywhere. It is fair to say their preparations for it under Bobby Robson were rather less scientific than they were under Gareth Southgate 34 years later, when all five of their players scored to send them through against Switzerland in the quarter-final of Euro 2024.

They had only started practising penalties at the end of the group stage, but Robson still felt they were ready. 'We had a plan,' he later recalled. 'Our regular penalty-taker Gary Lineker would give us the start we needed and we would save our next best, Stuart Pearce, for the crucial fourth spot-kick.'

So, Pearce waited and watched while Lineker, Peter Beardsley and David Platt beat Illgner to find the net for England, and Andreas Brehme, Lothar Matthäus and Karl-Heinz Riedle did the same against Peter Shilton for West Germany.

That left the score at 3–3 as Pearce, who was Nottingham Forest's regular spot-kick taker, walked forward from the halfway line to take his turn.

At this point, admittedly after only three attempts, England players had a 100 per cent success rate in shootouts and, commentating for ITV, Martin Tyler sounded confident that run would continue. 'England will feel pretty happy about Pearce coming up in this situation,' he says. 'A man who doesn't mince his words and really doesn't mess about when it comes to hitting a football.'

The England manager was optimistic too. 'If I had to back one player, it would be Pearce,' Robson remembered thinking. 'Cool, and with the hardest shot in the business.'

Pearce's power does not let him down, but his placement does. His shot is low and down the

Pearce celebrates after his free-kick put Nottingham Forest ahead in the 1991 FA Cup final. Tottenham won the game 2–1 after extra time.

middle of the goal and although Illgner has dived early, to his right, the ball cannons off his right foot and rebounds to safety.

'Our world caves in,' was Robson's reaction, and there is no rescue act. Olaf Thon scores West Germany's fourth penalty and they don't need to take their fifth because Chris Waddle has blasted England's next effort over the bar and into orbit somewhere over Turin.

Pearce immediately felt he had let his team-mates and his country down and, stranded in what he later described as 'a trance of misery', he was inconsolable on the pitch, then cried on the team coach as he left the stadium.

'You know how hard Stuart was, but he was in tears,' Lineker recalled in 2022. 'There was nothing I could say to him to make him feel better. In that scenario, you just put your arm on their shoulder. What do you say? "Oh, bad luck mate, don't worry about it, it's your fault that we are never going to gain footballing immortality." No, you just felt nothing but sympathy for him and Waddle.'

'You know how hard Stuart was, but he was in tears.'
– Gary Lineker

Pearce admits he put all the blame on himself in the aftermath, and did not get over the disappointment quickly. 'I would like to say it was easy, but it wasn't,' he revealed after his playing career was over – which makes what happened in that shootout against Spain at Wembley six years later even more special.

'It was not a moment I was waiting for, because I would rather we had won in 90 minutes,' he told the BBC in 2015. 'But I knew

Pearce made 522 appearances for Nottingham Forest in all competitions and managed the club twice.

if it went to penalties I would want to put myself forward and I knew by the time it went to extra-time, I had to go to the manager (Terry Venables) and tell him.

'So I went straight to him and told him I would take the third penalty, and he looked at me and went "Are you sure?" with an expletive in there, and I said "I was before you said that."'

Alan Shearer powerfully put England's first penalty away and they were handed the early advantage when Fernando Hierro slammed Spain's opener against the bar. Platt and Guillermo Amor both converted, meaning the score was 2–1 in England's favour when Pearce made that same lonely walk from the halfway line.

'A brave man steps forward to take England's third,' said Barry Davies on the BBC. 'Nobody really wants to see him miss it,' said ITV commentator Brian Moore. 'Stuart Pearce is stepping up to cleanse his soul,' added Tyler.

'We were all holding our breath,' said Shearer. Pearce knew why, but he was ready.

'Failure is not putting yourself forward,' he said later. 'Whatever comes, comes your way. I knew I was one of the five best penalty-takers still left on the pitch, but I felt as though there was more nerves in the stands than there probably was in me.'

This time, the result is relief rather than regret. Spain goalkeeper Andoni Zubizarreta guesses the right way but can do nothing to keep out a fierce drive into his left-hand corner. Then comes another reaction of raw emotion from Pearce, and it is the one everyone wants to see.

He throws a fist towards the sky then starts howling to the crowd, who are lost in the moment too. It was 'a penalty scored with a roar' as another commentator, Guy Mowbray, would later describe it, and the world can see just how much Pearce cares.

'It all came out,' Pearce said. 'I stopped for a second and then I turned to the crowd, who were going wild. They were screaming and I started screaming at them too – "come on, come on!" I was punching the air with my left fist, jutting out my chest, my chin was going. I had lost it.'

England, in contrast, would go on to win the shootout 4–2, although they would fall short in a shootout again soon afterwards, just four days later in fact, when they lost their semi-final to Germany on penalties.

Everyone remembers how Southgate's spot-kick was the one that cost them that time but, from Pearce's point of view, it is worth adding that he put away another penalty on this occasion too.

His demons were exorcised, that dragon was slain, but in any case his legacy was already assured – it would be his celebration against Spain that defined him in an England shirt, not his tears.

'It cemented my reputation among the supporters as one of them, I think,' Pearce told the BBC. 'It underlined my image as someone who would give everything for their country, because people would see it written on my face.

'Playing for England was at my core. I am not sure I was a psycho [as per his nickname for his uncompromising playing style and steely stare that was more like a glare] but I did want to give everything and I never wanted to show I was hurt.'

Those penalties alone made Pearce's passion public property but, if he had followed his childhood dreams, he might have been trying to save them instead. Gordon Banks was his first hero and he wanted to be a goalkeeper growing up – Banks's famous 1970 save from Pelé was his earliest memory.

Playing at Wembley was always an ambition, however. He had grown up around the corner in nearby Kingsbury, a couple of stops away on the London Underground, and worked in the bars there as a young teenager while watching greyhound racing and the speedway with his dad. He even saw the stuntman Evel Knievel when he jumped over 13 London buses there in 1975.

Still, getting on the hallowed turf himself must have seemed an ever more distant dream, the older he got. When he was 13, a letter from his father led to a trial with Queens Park Rangers, the same team he supported, but he was released after six months.

His future did not appear to be as a full-time footballer so instead a young Pearce thought about joining the police or the army. He passed physical tests with the latter with flying colours but was rejected after telling them he was waiting to see how he got on with the police the following week, and then promptly failed his interview with them too.

Pearce was left distraught after seeing his penalty saved during the shootout that decided the 1990 World Cup semi-final.

He was appreciated rather more by a different set of boys in blue, Wealdstone FC, whom he had joined after leaving secondary school in the spring of 1978 on the recommendation of the school's caretaker, Geoff Carson.

Pearce signed a two-year contract that paid him £15 a week and, shortly afterwards, made his first-team debut away at Dorchester at the age of 17, the first of his 242 games for the club.

He still needed a trade, however, and during a spell working in a warehouse as a spares clerk for television manufacturers Binatone, he began attending day-release classes to become a qualified electrician, before getting an apprenticeship, along with his brother Ray, to work for Brent Council.

For the next five years he changed fuses during the week, then stopped opposing wingers at the weekend, and for a spell he even went back in goal too, moonlighting for his mates' Sunday side, Dynamo Kingsbury Kiev, in the West Fulham and District League.

'I was a contracted non-league player so I had to use an assumed name,' Pearce explains. 'So I used to sign the team-sheet as my pseudonym, a Russian called Yak Jensen. I wore an orange and black kit with CCCP across both knee caps. I used to go up for every corner and take free-kicks on the edge of the opposition box.'

It is a bizarre scenario but it only ended when Pearce suffered a serious injury while playing for Kiev. Not for the last time, he tried to play through the pain.

Pearce's bravery was evident when he stepped up to take another spot-kick six years after his World Cup anguish, against Spain in the quarter-final of Euro '96.

Pearce . . . quickly built a reputation as a reliable and tough-tackling left-back.

'I'd come out to the edge of my area and some kid had kicked me on the side of the leg,' Pearce said. 'It was a bit sore but I didn't think anything more of it. On the Saturday, Wealdstone played Runcorn away and I went out for the warm-up and as I was running I heard this sort of "slap" noise and it felt as though someone had thrown a lump of mud at my leg.

'What had actually happened is that I had started to break a small bone in my shin the previous weekend, and now it had completely gone. I said to the manager "I think I've broken my leg or something," and he said "give it five minutes and see how you get on, try to run it off."

'I did that but it was no good and I had to come off. I went for a scan on my leg the following day and saw the damage, and that was the end of Yak Jensen.'

It was probably just as well. Pearce had rejected an approach from one Football League side, third-tier Hull City, early in his Wealdstone career but the next professional club to come calling were a top flight team, Coventry City, and this was too good an opportunity to pass up.

When the Sky Blues paid Wealdstone £25,000 to sign Pearce in 1983 he was catapulted into the big time, at the age of 21, with a two-year contract worth £250 a week – although his boss at Brent Council said he would keep his old job open if things did not work out for him as a professional footballer.

Pearce did not need to take him up on the offer. It was a big step up from non-league to Division One but Pearce took it in his stride, and quickly built a reputation as a reliable and tough-tackling left-back.

His rapid upward trajectory continued two years later when Brian Clough took him to Nottingham Forest in a joint deal worth £450,000 with fellow defender Ian Butterworth. By now, Pearce was established at the top level, and was quickly made Forest skipper, but he was still working as an electrician in his spare time.

He asked Clough for permission to put an advert in the Forest match-day programme offering his services, and his manager agreed – on the

Pearce's celebration after scoring against Spain is one of the most famous in Three Lions' history.

condition he fixed a faulty iron and mended a broken kettle for him.

The ad read: 'Stuart Pearce electrician. Repairs and maintenance. All work guaranteed. Complete household rewires. Estimates free' and it was still running when he got his first call-up from his country, as an over-aged Under-21 player, against Yugoslavia in autumn 1986.

Pearce made it into Bobby Robson's senior squad a few months later, to face Brazil and Scotland in the Rous Cup in May 1987. He was thrilled, but Clough quickly brought him back down to earth when he asked him into his office.

'I thought he was going to give me a big pat on the back and a wage rise that kind of thing. I'm his captain, he'll be so pleased I've been picked for England,' Pearce said. 'But I walked in and he said "I see you're in the England squad, do you think you're good enough?" I said "I'm not sure" and he went "I don't. Get out!"'

Clough meant it, by the way, and others were undecided about Pearce too. 'Some people in football harboured doubts about my playing style and said that the way I tackled and the aggression I showed would be a problem in the international game,' Pearce later recalled. He would go on to prove them all wrong.

Although his debut, as the 999th player to represent his country, did not exactly go to plan when Brazil winger Müller lost him to set up their equaliser in a 1–1 draw. He kept his place and only missed out on the 1988 European Championship because of injury. He would soon replace Kenny Sansom as first-choice.

'By the time the 1990 World Cup came around, I had already won 24 caps,' Pearce wrote in his 2020 book. 'When the tournament began, I was ready.'

The way it ended would leave Pearce wounded emotionally, but rather than feeling sorry for himself he used the abuse he received the following season as a spark to improve his game. 'Everywhere I went, I had opposition fans yelling "Pearce is a German" at me,' he said. 'But it really didn't bother me. It motivated me, if anything.'

Pearce scored 16 goals in all competitions in 1990–91 and was shortlisted for the Professional Footballers' Association's Player of the Year award. He also helped Forest reach the FA Cup final and book a return to Wembley, where he had lifted the League Cup in each of the two previous campaigns, but he did not get his hands on the trophy this time.

After putting Forest ahead with a fierce free-kick following the foul on Gary Charles that saw Paul Gascoigne sustain a serious injury, he could not prevent Tottenham fighting back to win 2–1 in extra-time.

Things initially went much better with England, who did not lose any of their first 12 games under new manager Graham Taylor, who had succeeded Robson following the World Cup. When they were finally beaten, by a newly unified Germany team at Wembley in September 1991, Pearce was absent through injury.

That was actually Taylor's only defeat in his first 21 games leading up to the 1992 European Championship, but those finals would end up being a huge let-down with England failing to register a single victory in Sweden and going out in the group stage after going down 2–1 to the hosts.

Pearce probably came closer than anyone to supplying a different narrative when he smashed a free-kick against the bar in England's second game, a drab 0–0 draw with France, while sporting a huge gash on his cheek after being head-butted by Basile Boli.

His reaction to that assault by Boli showed the calm head that lay behind Pearce's fearsome reputation, because he used the incident to intimidate the player he was marking, Jocelyn Angloma, instead of taking revenge.

'The last thing I wanted to do was to chase an opponent, throw a punch, and get sent off,' Pearce said later. 'Instead I turned on the unsuspecting Angloma and said "that was you, I'm going to kill you." He was frightened to death, thus making my job a lot easier.'

Pearce took over as captain for the qualifying campaign for the 1994 World Cup, but that ended in more misery, with his own worst moment coming after just 8.3 seconds of their final match against San Marino when his under-hit back-pass allowed Davide Gualtieri to run in and score. England recovered to win 7–1, but they were out.

That could have been his final act for his country – Taylor's replacement, Terry Venables, told him he would not be continuing either as skipper or as his first-choice left-back but, rather than retire from international football, Pearce played on.

That decision was rewarded when Graeme Le Saux was injured before Euro '96 and Pearce was restored to the team. He would also play under the next two England managers, Glenn Hoddle and Kevin Keegan, before a broken leg sustained while playing for West Ham finally brought the curtain down on his Three Lions career.

Pearce's final game for his country came in a goalless draw with Poland in September 1999, at the age of 37 years and 137 days. Stanley Matthews and Leslie Compton are England's only two outfield players who have been older.

By then Pearce had already tasted management in a brief spell as player-boss of Forest in 1997, before extending his club career with Newcastle, the Hammers and finally Manchester City, where he had the chance to score his 100th career goal with a stoppage-time penalty in his final match, against Portsmouth at the age of 39 in 2002. He missed the target from the spot for the first time in his career.

He later managed City before a six-year spell in charge of the England Under-21 side from 2007

Pearce went to the 2010 World Cup as one of Fabio Capello's assistants.

to 2013, during which time he also took charge of the Great Britain Olympic team at the 2012 games and worked with the senior side as a coach under Fabio Capello. When Capello left in 2012, Pearce took over as caretaker boss for one game, a 3–2 defeat by the Netherlands at Wembley.

He later returned to the City Ground for a longer, if unsuccessful, spell in charge of Forest, and coached another of his former clubs, West Ham, in two spells between 2017 and 2022.

Pearce, who is now working as a radio pundit, did not win many medals on the pitch or in the dugout, but he left his mark on the game in other ways.

'People come up to me in the street and say "why can't people play with the same passion for England as you, how can you put that into them?"' Pearce said in 2015. 'And I would say you can't put it into someone, they have got to have it inside of them from the offset.

'I was fortunate, in my mind anyway, that I have got that in me – that it means everything to represent my country at something, anything, and I just happened to be good enough at football.'

Bobby Dazzler – Bobby Charlton was widely regarded as the best player on the planet when England won the 1966 World Cup and is remembered as one of his sport's all-time greats.

5

BOBBY CHARLTON

Born	11 October 1937; died 21 October 2023
Place of birth	Ashington, Northumberland
Position	Midfielder

Bobby Charlton played 106 games for England between 1958 and 1970, including a key role in winning the 1966 World Cup, when he was described as 'the linchpin' by manager Alf Ramsey. He scored 49 goals for his country – a record that stood for 45 years until it was broken by Wayne Rooney in 2015. A Manchester United legend, Charlton captained his club to their European Cup triumph in 1968, 10 years after surviving the Munich air disaster. 'As near perfection as man and player as it is possible to be,' said his long-time manager at United, Sir Matt Busby.

Bobby Charlton was not just one of the greatest footballers England has ever produced, he was also among the most famous, successful and popular players and sporting personalities on the planet during a lifetime in the game that saw him experience tragedy as well as triumph, as the driving force for his club and country.

An attacking midfielder with a trademark long-range thunderbolt shot, Charlton had a reputation for supreme sportsmanship to match his immense ability, but his honesty did not diminish his passion, determination or bravery.

He was a superstar footballer, icon and ambassador for Manchester United and England, winning the European Cup, World Cup and Ballon d'Or, and becoming a symbol for old-fashioned English sportsmanship

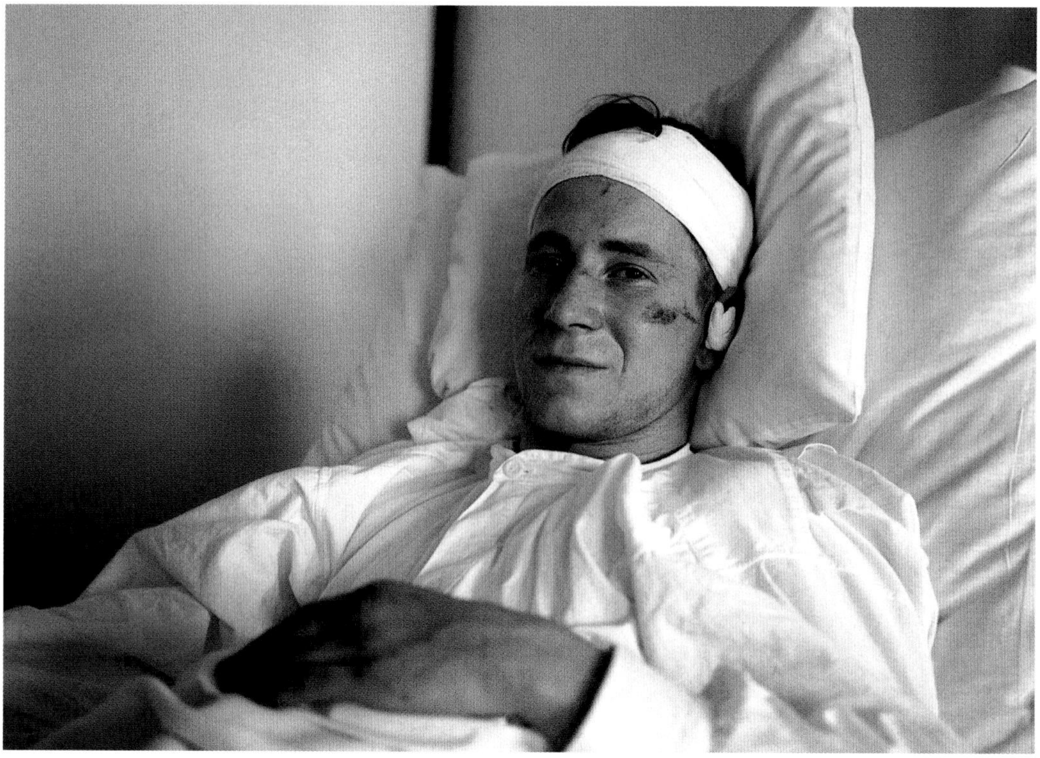

Charlton suffered head injuries in the Munich air disaster and spent a week in a German hospital.

– in the days when that mattered – but his career, and indeed his life, will forever be framed by the Munich air disaster, which gave added poignancy to everything that followed.

Charlton was part of a young and supremely talented United side – nicknamed the Busby Babes after their eponymous manager Matt Busby – who had become champions of England in 1957. On 6 February 1958, they were returning from a European Cup tie in Belgrade, having just beaten Yugoslavian side Red Star to advance to the semi-finals.

After stopping to refuel at Munich-Riem Airport, their plane – British European Airways Flight 609 – crashed on its third attempt to take off from a runway covered with snow and slush, and burst into flames.

Charlton, then aged 20, was thrown 40 yards clear of the burning wreckage and was found unconscious in a pool of water by United's goalkeeper Harry Gregg, who assumed he was dead.

'I remember us hitting a perimeter fence, and then I don't remember,' Charlton told a BBC documentary marking the 50th anniversary of the disaster in 2008. 'I heard clatters and bangs and then I woke up, I don't know how long later. Harry said I was out for maybe 10 or 15 minutes.'

A total of 23 people died in the crash, including eight of Charlton's team-mates: Geoff Bent, Roger Byrne, Eddie Colman, Mark Jones, David Pegg, Tommy Taylor, Billy Whelan and Duncan Edwards, who died in hospital 15 days later.

The loss of Edwards, his close friend and hero, plunged Charlton into deeper despair and led him to contemplate giving up the game. He would be back playing within a month, but the psychological scars of the trauma never fully healed.

Charlton would later say a day never passed by without him thinking of those who perished and, in his 2007 autobiography, he wrote: 'All the time the question came pounding in: Why me, why did I survive when the others didn't?'

Looking back in 2008, he said: 'It was just a monumental thing for a football club, for football in this country. It was just such a tragedy that so many young players were killed, and even more so that they were killed representing England, representing their country, representing their club and representing the city. And suddenly it was just stopped. Young players with the world at their feet, and suddenly no more.'

It was left to Charlton to fulfil their dreams as well as his own potential, and his recovery to help rebuild United before captaining them to their European Cup triumph of 1968 was remarkable enough. On top of that, he also played a key role in his country's finest moment on a football field and the mental fortitude he possessed along with his famed finesse was surely integral to all of that success.

As a player he was comfortable using either foot, showing supreme balance on the ball, and the same could be said about his temperament – his conduct was impeccable throughout his career.

All of these qualities were apparent from Charlton's early years as a brilliant boy prodigy in Ashington, a Northumberland coal mining village, after he was born into a famous footballing family from the north-east.

His grandfather and four of his uncles were professionals and his mother, Cissie, was obsessed with the game – her cousin was

> 'I dreamt of being a footballer – my whole family was football mad.'
> – *Bobby Charlton*

Jackie Milburn, who starred for Newcastle and England – and Charlton quickly realised he wanted to follow in their footsteps.

'I dreamt of being a footballer – my whole family was football mad,' Charlton told the BBC in a programme marking his 80th birthday in 2017. 'When they used to come home for the weekend, occasionally they would come down the park and we would have a little kickaround and I thought, this is what I want. I could see them signing autographs and I thought that must be great.'

Charlton had started off playing with his older brother – another future England World Cup winner, Jack – in the street using a tennis ball and it would not be long before his own career took off.

His ability as an all-rounder caught the eye and 18 different clubs tried to sign him, but it was Manchester United who snapped him up after their scout, Joe Armstrong, spotted him playing for East Northumberland Schools on a frozen pitch in Jarrow.

When Charlton left school at 15, he headed for Old Trafford, signing his first contract with the club on New Year's Day 1953 and giving up an apprenticeship as an electrical engineer to turn professional on his 17th birthday in October 1954.

Under Busby and his assistant Jimmy Murphy, United's devotion to developing talented young players made them the perfect fit for Charlton and his early promise soon translated into trophies – he helped United win the FA Youth Cup three seasons running in 1954, 1955 and 1956 – as well as a chance in United's first team. He was picked to face Charlton Athletic aged 18 on 6 October 1956 and marked it with two goals in a 4–2 win.

'Jimmy turned me from an amateur schoolboy player into a professional player, and it took about two years,' Charlton told BBC series *Kicking and Screaming* in 1994. 'Whenever he got the opportunity he used to pull me to one side and try to teach me the folly of trying to make impossible passes, when there was something more realistic you can do, more beneficial to the team. He made me think more as a team player rather than as an individual, but

Charlton waves to the crowd at Stamford Bridge after his final game for Manchester United in April 1973.

nevertheless always encouraged me to make the best of the assets I had.'

Murphy's advice would help Charlton make an impact for England as well as United. International honours came early too, and he represented his country at schoolboy, youth and Under-23 levels before being handed his first full cap against Scotland in April 1958 at the age of 20, just two months after being dragged to safety on that runway in Munich.

Again he found the net, meeting Tom Finney's cross with a peach of a volley from near the penalty spot, in a convincing 4–0 win at Hampden Park and more goals followed against Portugal at Wembley a fortnight later. Two fierce finishes gave England a 2–1 win, and by now the power of his shots was attracting attention from admirers in the press and public alike.

That bright start did not last long, however. Charlton was much less impressive in a 5–0 defeat by a fast and clever Yugoslavia side in England's next game and it cost him his place in the team – although he made the squad for that summer's World Cup finals, he did not feature in Sweden.

Footballing brothers Bobby (left) and Jack Charlton played together 28 times for England, including every minute of all six games at the 1966 World Cup.

At this stage of his career he was still something of an enigma and his occasionally spectacular contributions were not enough to fully earn the trust of England manager Walter Winterbottom or, crucially, the national team's selection committee.

It was only when Charlton switched positions from left winger to an attacking central midfield role, that he began to deliver consistently, earning him the nickname 'Bobby Dazzler'. He excelled as England reached the quarter-finals of the next World Cup in 1962 and his growing maturity was fully rewarded when Alf Ramsey took over as England manager a few months later.

With Ramsey, England finally had a manager fully in charge of picking the team and its tactics, and as the 1966 World Cup approached he implemented a style that suited Charlton's game and his intelligence, allowing him to drop deeper and orchestrate play as well as bursting forward to let fly with his trademark shots.

Charlton's form for United had already brought individual accolades – shortly before the tournament began he was named England's Footballer of the Year and also collected the coveted Ballon d'Or, awarded to Europe's best player – and now he was targeting the greatest prize of all.

England were the hosts, and also among the favourites. A run of nine wins and one draw meant confidence and expectations were high going into their opening match in Group One, but they could find no way through Uruguay's massed defence and it finished 0–0.

They needed something or someone to kickstart their campaign in their next game, against Mexico, and it was Charlton who delivered, in typical blockbuster style, just before half-time.

There seemed no obvious danger when he picked up the ball in his own half but a jinking run took him to the edge of the Mexico box, where he shifted the ball to his right foot and had only one thing on his mind.

'I remember Jimmy Murphy used to say, "don't be afraid to shoot,"' Charlton recalled. 'The public will always forgive you if you shoot and you miss, but they will never forgive you if you don't shoot.

'The Mexicans were defending but there was some space in between and I got the ball and I carried it. Eventually I got to about 30 yards out and the ball just was running smoothly and I just thought if he [the defender] lets me go, I am going to hit it. I smashed it . . . and it was as sweet as a nut.'

It was the sort of unstoppable strike Charlton is remembered for. Mexico keeper Ignacio Calderón had no chance as the ball rocketed into the top corner of the net and England's World Cup was up and running at last. Roger Hunt made it 2–0 with 15 minutes to go, and the win meant they had one foot in the quarter-finals.

'Suddenly England were maybe back on the rails again,' Charlton added. 'Afterwards, people used to tell me that they wanted to back us, but they needed a little bit of something, you know, and they said this goal just got us on our path, and that was just sensational.'

There was more of the same to come in the semi-finals, where Charlton again stepped up to supply two more goals of equal importance in a classic encounter with an exciting Portugal side.

His first came with half an hour gone, when Roger Hunt ran on to a hoisted Ray Wilson pass and Portugal keeper José Pereira slid out to intercept, using his knees to knock the ball clear as far as the edge of the area – where Charlton was perfectly positioned to fire it back past him.

'It came straight back to me, because I'd been going up to help support,' said Charlton. 'I remembered when I was a schoolboy playing at Wembley how smooth it was, and I trusted the pitch and I passed the ball into the goal.'

Portugal poured forward in the second half in search of an equaliser but England survived a wave of attacks and it fell to Charlton to round off a superb team move and make it 2–0 with 10 minutes to go.

One of Charlton's trademark fierce shots from distance put England 2–0 up in their 1966 semi-final against Portugal.

'I teed it up,' said Geoff Hurst. 'And of course he wasn't going to miss from about 15 yards with the power he had in his shot.'

Charlton is actually a little further away, on the edge of the area, when he meets the ball but it makes no difference. Like his opening goal of the game, he hits it first time, but this time it is with full force.

'He just knocked the ball right in front of me, and I didn't even have to break stride,' Charlton explained. 'I hit it and I knew I had scored as soon as I had hit it. The ball flew into the other corner and we had done it, we were in the final.'

Even then, Charlton showed his compassionate side. When Portugal's star player Eusébio, who had scored a late consolation from the penalty spot, broke down and wept openly on the final whistle, Charlton was one of the first to console him.

'He is that kind of person,' Eusébio said afterwards. 'It broke my heart to lose that match and I could do nothing to stop the tears coming. But if Portugal had to lose, I'm glad we lost to a team containing Bobby Charlton.'

And so to the World Cup final. As we now know, the biggest day in England's footballing history also provided their greatest triumph, but Charlton did not play the kind of role in their victory that he or anyone else had expected, especially given what he had done to get them there.

Told by a TV reporter on the eve of the game that the Germans considered him their main threat, he replied, 'I hope I prove them right', but Ramsey had other plans for him, involving Germany's star man, 20-year-old Franz Beckenbauer.

'Alf said to me "I want you to mark Beckenbauer, and don't let him out of your sight,"' Charlton recalled. 'And that was it really. I thought well, I have waited my whole life to play in a World Cup final . . . and I am asked to man-mark, which I have never done before.'

It turned out he was not the only one given those instructions. Beckenbauer was also ordered to follow Charlton around because his manager, Helmut Schön, regarded him as 'the engine of England's game'. As soon as the whistle went to start the game, he ran over to Charlton and the two shadowed each other all game, meaning neither had much impact on the outcome.

'It was interesting really in that final that two of the greatest players I have ever played with and against virtually cancelled each other out,' Geoff Hurst would reflect. 'Bobby never complained about that and the fact that never once did he shirk that duty, again showed his character and his personality.'

All of his emotions were on display too. When Hurst completed his hat-trick at the end of extra-time to seal England's famous 4–2 win, Charlton and his brother Jack both collapsed in tears on the Wembley turf.

'I remember going on my knees and thinking "thank god for that",' Jack said. 'Then I bumped into our Robert and I just gave him a hug.'

'He said to me, "well what about that, kidda, what about that?"' Bobby explained. 'I started crying, I only ever cried when we won, and I said to him "Jackie, our lives are never going to be the same again."

'We knew that we had done something that will never ever happen again here, in our lives. And we had a long time in our careers to play football and to win other things, but I think to be the best team in the world was just magic. It is something that I will always remember, doing your absolute best, and I can't do any more.'

England had conquered the world, and this was a golden period for Manchester United too, with Charlton joined by Denis Law and George Best to form a legendary attacking triumvirate known as 'the Holy Trinity'.

Together they won league titles in 1965 and 1967 and would be back at Wembley on 29 May 1968 to help Charlton win the only major trophy he was missing, the European Cup.

United had overcome six-time winners Real Madrid in the semi-finals, meaning that 10 years after Munich, they had made it to their first final, where they would face Portuguese champions Benfica.

It would turn out to be an unforgettable night, particularly for Charlton who scored the first and last goals in a famous 4–1 win after extra-time, and again sank to his knees on the Wembley turf when it was all over.

'I remember everyone was jumping up and cheering,' Charlton said. 'We'd done it. When the final whistle went, everyone dashed to Sir Matt. They were his players that had been lost in Munich, they were his lads, his team.

'I think everyone in the whole crowd, maybe even in the whole country, thought a little bit about his feelings that night. He had started it off, and now he had seen it through. It didn't seem right that Manchester United had never won the European Cup, but that became the standard.'

Although he stayed at Old Trafford for five more years, patrolling midfield with his signature combover hairstyle, the decline of Busby's team meant further club success eluded Charlton.

There were more highlights to come at international level, however, for example when he captained England for the first time in January 1969, on his 91st appearance, a 1–1 draw with Romania at Wembley, and also when he marked his 100th cap with a goal against Northern Ireland in April 1970, but his England career did not get a happy ending either.

At that summer's World Cup, Charlton's fourth, he was still an integral part of Ramsey's midfield, but at 32 his game time in the stifling heat and high altitude in Mexico had to be managed, and there was to be no repeat of 1966, when he had played every minute of the campaign.

He captained England for the first time in January 1969, on his 91st appearance . . .

Charlton started all three of England's group games, against Romania, Brazil and Czechoslovakia, but was substituted in the latter two matches, firstly for Alan Ball and then for Colin Bell – one of the innovations of this tournament was to allow replacements for the first time, and here they were used tactically rather than following injuries.

West Germany were waiting in the quarter-finals, in what was another epic encounter to match the final from four years ago. It started well for England, who were playing some fabulous football and went 2–0 up with goals from Alan Mullery and Martin Peters.

Legend has it that Ramsey then decided to take Charlton off to save his legs for the semi-final but Beckenbauer had already pulled a goal back by the time he made his subs with less than 20 minutes to go, and it seems more likely he was trying to shore up his defence by bringing on the younger Bell for Charlton and another defender, Norman Hunter, for the more attack-minded Peters.

Charlton lifts the European Cup in 1968. He became the first player to win the World Cup, Ballon d'Or and European Cup.

Whatever the reason for the switch, it failed. Uwe Seeler equalised with a clever back-header from Karl-Heinz Schnellinger's cross, and in extra-time Gerd Müller volleyed West Germany's winner.

Debate has raged ever since whether Charlton's departure cost England, with the team's captain Bobby Moore among those to question the decision.

'Alf has taken stick for those substitutions but at the moment he was putting Norman and Colin on, it seemed right,' Moore said in his 1976 biography.

'You figured he was thinking it was worth sparing Bobby because the semi-final was only three days away. Bobby was no youngster and it would have looked bad if such a key player was jaded

Charlton presents Wayne Rooney with his 100th England cap in November 2014.

after an unnecessary 20 minutes in that heat. Norman seemed ideal for making sure we locked them out and Bellie was strong, powerful. Just the man to run a beaten team into the ground.

'But when you thought about it, Bobby was one of the fittest men in the squad. Always had been. Loved to play and could play all day in an oven if you asked him. You could tell Bobby didn't want to go off and as soon as he walked away it was like a ton weight had been lifted off Beckenbauer.

'They hadn't had a kick at the ball for 70 minutes and suddenly Franz starts coming at us for the first time.'

It is typical of Charlton that he never criticised his manager's decision himself. Although he admitted to being 'distraught' while watching West Germany's fightback from the bench, he would subsequently agree with Ramsey that the absence of regular goalkeeper Banks through illness played a much bigger part in why things went wrong.

England's defence of their title was over, and so was Charlton's international career – he retired the next day after a conversation with Ramsey, who told him he would be too old for his team by the time the next World Cup came around.

His final appearance had seen him set a new mark for most caps, 106, and he had also scored the most goals with 49. That stood until 2015 and the man who beat it, Wayne Rooney, also broke Charlton's record of 249 goals for Manchester United in 2017.

After two decades and 758 appearances – another record he held until Ryan Giggs passed it in 2008 – Charlton left United in 1973 but his next move, a foray into management with Preston North End, was not a success.

His first season saw them relegated into the third tier and although he then returned as a player, he could not improve their fortunes significantly and he stepped down at the end of his second campaign. Other than a brief spell as caretaker manager of Wigan Athletic in 1983, he would not return to the dugout.

Instead he was back at his beloved United as a director in 1984, and would remain a fixture at the club for the rest of his life, a trusted adviser to managers including Sir Alex Ferguson. The club named Old Trafford's south stand in his honour in 2016 and he is immortalised outside the ground by the bronze Holy Trinity statue which also features Best and Law.

Charlton also worked as an international ambassador for the Football Association and ran a network of successful youth coaching schools, which discovered David Beckham and helped bring him to United. They became close friends.

After being awarded the OBE in 1969 and the CBE in 1974, Charlton was knighted in 1994. He rarely missed a United match in his later years until he was diagnosed with dementia in 2020. He died in 2023, aged 86.

David Beckham is a global cultural phenomenon, but he is also one of the most decorated players in football history.

6

DAVID BECKHAM

Born	2 May 1975
Place of birth	Leytonstone, London
Position	Midfielder

David Beckham played 115 games for England between 1996 and 2009. He scored 17 goals for his country and captained the national side on 59 occasions. He played at three World Cups, scoring at each tournament, and is the only Englishman to have won league titles in four different countries – England, Spain, the United States and France – including six Premier League titles with Manchester United.

From public enemy number one in 1998 to national hero in 2001, David Beckham's England journey was a unique one, but that part of his story is testimony to the resilience that was as much a trademark of his entire career for club and country as his famous free-kicks.

There were plenty of headlines along the way too, of course, covering more than just the highs and lows of his life in football.

For the past 100 years, many England players have traded on their status with commercial deals and monetised their stardom but none of them quite transcended sport the way Beckham did to become a global cultural phenomenon and fashion icon.

From *Bend it Like Beckham* to 'Brand Beckham', his fame seemed to know no limits but not everyone thought the way he embraced the celebrity circus and courted the camera when he started dating his now-wife, Spice Girls singer Victoria Adams, in early 1997 was conducive to success on the pitch.

Beckham celebrates after scoring his last-gasp free-kick against Greece that sent England to the 2002 World Cup.

His long-time Manchester United mentor Sir Alex Ferguson wrote in his 2013 autobiography that Beckham was the only player he managed who chose to be famous, which was one of the reasons he sold him to Real Madrid in 2003 after a very public fall-out.

There is much more to Beckham than just hype, however. His interest in his image cannot be denied, but neither can his drive and determination. He was never a prima donna on the pitch and his professionalism as a player kept him at the highest level for more than two decades and saw him lift trophies wherever he played.

While you would never describe him as being as naturally gifted as, say, Paul Gascoigne, or possessing the explosive pace and trickery of John Barnes at his peak, Beckham made the absolute most of the talent he did have.

As well as his deserved reputation for distinctive dead-ball deliveries and swerving shots from distance, he honed an exceptional technique that gave his right foot a remarkable passing range in open play, including those wonderful whipped crosses.

Those qualities, on top of his amazing work ethic and superb stamina when his team were out of possession, were instilled at an early age. 'Practice makes perfect' was the mantra of his dad, Ted, a self-employed gasfitter who regularly worked 12-hour days before taking David to a park near their home in Chingford, east London, to put him through his paces.

Day after day, week after week, Ted was a hard taskmaster, starting from when David was six. He would repeatedly ask his son to hit the crossbar of one of the goals for hours on end, offering him 50p as a prize every time he managed it.

'Without a doubt, it was tough love,' Beckham told the BBC in 2021. 'I remember being seven years old, playing for my local side Ridgeway Rovers on a Sunday morning and if I had a bad game Dad would tell me – and he would go through every single minute, every minute detail, of that game, on the way home. I remember turning around to him sometimes and saying I was so sorry, that I didn't mean to, but, when I look back now, that was exactly how I needed to be taught.'

Ted gave him more than discipline, he also passed on his love of Manchester United – one of Beckham's middle names is Robert after his hero, Bobby Charlton – and his dad's passion would play a big part in the path David took when people began to notice his ability.

After seeing an advert for Bobby Charlton Soccer Schools in the north-west, Ted enrolled his then 10-year-old son during the summer holidays and put him in lodgings in Manchester for a fortnight. Beckham went back the following year and won the skills competition, the final of which took place on the Old Trafford pitch. The prize was a trip to train with Barcelona and Beckham got to meet their manager Terry Venables and British stars Gary Lineker, Steve Archibald and Mark Hughes, but it was also the start of a lasting connection with United that would soon become a formal arrangement.

A few months later, Beckham was playing in an Under-12 representative game for his area, Waltham Forest, against neighbouring Redbridge. With Ted at work, his mum Sandra was present, and was approached afterwards by a teacher, Malcolm Fidgeon, who had been one of United's scouts in London since 1966, to say he wanted to take Beckham up to Manchester for a trial.

'I burst into tears because it was all I ever wanted,' Beckham recalled. 'I had other offers – West Ham, Wimbledon and Arsenal were all interested, and I was training with Tottenham because my grandad was a season ticket holder there for 40 years. Manchester United were my dad's team, though, and they were my team too. This was my opportunity.'

Spurs still tried to persuade him to join them instead, but Beckham's mind was made up. He signed his first contract for United aged 14 and moved up to train with them when he left school a couple of years later.

Under the guidance of United's legendary youth coach, Eric Harrison, Beckham joined a crop of talented prospects including Ryan Giggs, Paul Scholes, brothers Gary and Phil Neville, and Nicky Butt who would eventually be feted as the famed 'Class of 92', named after the year they won the prestigious FA Youth Cup. They still had to fight for their big chance, however.

Beckham made his senior debut for United when he came off the bench at the age of 17 in a League Cup tie against Brighton in September 1992, but did not get any more first-team action for almost two years and began to have doubts about his future prospects when he spent time on loan with Preston in 1994–95.

It was the following campaign where he began to make his mark, as part of the young United team that were dismissed by BBC pundit Alan Hansen after a disastrous opening-day defeat.

Speaking on *Match of the Day* after United had been beaten 3–1 by Aston Villa in a game which saw Beckham score his first Premier League goal, host Des Lynam said 'United were scarcely recognisable from the team we've known over the last couple of seasons, what's going on?'

Hansen famously replied, 'You can't win anything with kids . . . the trick of winning the championship is having strength in depth and they just haven't got it.'

These kids were different, however. They went on to do the Double of Premier League and FA Cup, and it was Beckham's corner that led to Eric Cantona's late winner against Liverpool at Wembley.

At this stage, Beckham was still not a household name but his fame sky-rocketed on the first day of the following season, when he scored from the halfway line in a win over Wimbledon at Selhurst Park.

'Absolutely phenomenal' was how commentator John Motson

Beckham helped raise money for the Manchester United Foundation when he played in a Legends match against Bayern Munich in 2019, on the 20th anniversary of United's Treble success.

From United to the Galacticos – Beckham left Old Trafford for Real Madrid in 2003.

summed up the strike and it is spectacular by any standards, with Beckham spotting goalkeeper Neil Sullivan slightly off his line and letting fly with a looping shot that dips under the crossbar, to the delight of the travelling United fans behind the goal.

'I remember Pelé trying it in 1970,' Ferguson exclaimed afterwards. 'Many players have tried it, but I don't think I've seen it done before.'

Suddenly Beckham had superstar status. 'That was the moment he came to the fore and was noticed by everyone,' Gary Lineker reflected later. 'To do something as precocious as that made him look a bit different.'

A fortnight after that, Beckham's full international debut followed, in a 3–0 World Cup qualifying win over Moldova in Glenn Hoddle's first game in charge. Still only 21, he became a regular as England secured a place at the 1998 World Cup, including starting a vital and hard-fought 0–0 draw with Italy in Rome.

So it was something of a surprise when Beckham was left out of England's opening match of the finals in France, a 2–0 win over Tunisia. When he asked Hoddle why he was dropped, Beckham was told 'I don't think you're focused.'

Although he soon forced his way back into the team for their final group match, a must-win game against Colombia, and sealed England's 2–0 win with his first international goal, one of those terrific curling free-kicks, his tournament ended in disgrace when he was sent off against Argentina in the last 16.

The game, at Stade Geoffroy-Guichard, Saint-Ètienne, on 30 June, had started well enough for Beckham, who played the through-ball for Michael Owen to run in and score his brilliant goal to put England 2–1 up, but Argentina equalised before the break and, just after half-time, Beckham was barged over by Diego Simeone.

Beckham recalled what happened next in his 2003 autobiography, where he wrote: 'He clattered me from behind. Then, while I was down on the ground, he made as if to ruffle my hair and gave it a tug.

'I flicked my leg up backwards towards him. It was instinctive, but the wrong thing to do. You just can't allow yourself to retaliate. I was provoked but, almost at the same moment I reacted, I knew I shouldn't have done. Of course, Simeone went down as if he'd been shot.'

Anger and abuse followed him everywhere he went the following season, apart from Old Trafford . . .

Danish referee Kim Milton Nielsen, who was right on the scene, did not hesitate before brandishing a red card at Beckham. England drew the game but lost on penalties and while the punishment appeared harsh – Gary Lineker would later say 'I can't believe he sent him off for what was basically an

Posh and Becks – David and Victoria Beckham are football's most famous celebrity couple.

innocuous little flick' – it was soon clear who the scapegoat was.

'Moment of lunacy that cost Cup hopes' was the *Daily Mail* front page, while 'Ten heroic lions, one stupid boy' screamed the headline in the *Daily Mirror*, who went a step further a few days later when they offered readers a cut-out dartboard with Beckham's head at the centre of it, accompanied by the text: Still bitter? Take your fury out.

Things got worse, not better, in the weeks that followed as the English press went into meltdown and they were not the only ones to target him. Beckham, who had found out during the tournament that Victoria was pregnant with their first child, received death threats and bullets in the post. Hate mobs hounded his family and an effigy of him was even put in a noose and hung outside a south London pub.

Anger and abuse followed him everywhere he went the following season, apart from Old Trafford, where he received a standing ovation from United fans every time he took a corner. The club had stood by him and Ferguson had been quick to offer support.

'How did I get through it? My family, Manchester United and Sir Alex Ferguson,' Beckham told the BBC in 2021.

'The first person to call me after that game was Sir Alex, who said "son, get back to Manchester, you'll be fine" and that gave me strength to actually get through probably the toughest time that I've been through in my life, in my career.

'I didn't realise how bad it was going to be and how bad it was going to get until I was getting a connecting flight after landing back in England with the team, and as I was walking through the airport, a journalist and a camera crew were following me and said, "How do you feel? You've let your family down, your nation down, and your grandparents down."

'It should have been a happy time, with us expecting our first child. It wasn't but I knew back in Manchester I'd be protected, and that I had the support of the fans.'

Beckham repaid that backing by helping United clinch a historic Treble the following season, and he took both corners that led to goals in their incredible late fightback to beat Bayern Munich in the 1999 Champions League final, the same year he was runner-up in the Ballon d'Or.

He took longer to win back the affections of England fans

Beckham was sent off by Danish referee Kim Milton Nielsen after kicking out at Argentina's Diego Simeone at the 1998 World Cup.

who continued to taunt him – there was another backlash after he reacted to boos and abusive chants throughout a defeat by Portugal at Euro 2000 by raising his middle finger towards supporters afterwards – and that was also typical of the toxic treatment he still received from the terraces at away games while playing for United.

At that stage, Beckham was still known as the most hated man in England and that, plus the regular intrusion into his personal life by the British newspapers, even led him to consider a move abroad to escape the unwanted attention.

He stuck it out however, and the public's perception of him began to change when caretaker boss Peter Taylor made him England captain for a friendly against Italy later that year.

Beckham kept the armband under new manager Sven-Göran Eriksson and starred in a glorious 5–1 win over Germany in Munich in autumn 2001 – the first time they had beaten them since 1966 – that put England top of their qualifying group for the 2002 World Cup.

They only needed to match Germany's draw against Finland in the final game of their campaign, at home against Greece on 6 October 2001, to finish the job and book their ticket to Japan and South Korea, but that looked beyond them as the game entered stoppage time, with England trailing 2–1.

In the 93rd minute it was Beckham who saved them, at Old Trafford of all places, capping a superb individual performance in trademark style with a stunning 30-yard free-kick into the top corner.

'David Beckham has done it. It had to be Beckham!' – *Alan Green*

'Up and over the wall . . . and in,' screamed BBC Radio 5 Live commentator Alan Green. 'David Beckham has done it. It had to be Beckham!'

The goal sparked wild celebrations at his home stadium and completed his transformation from villain to national hero.

'That was the moment that England fans forgave me for what had happened a few years before,' he would later say. 'For me personally, that was redemption for what had happened, because up until then, there was always that cloud around the sending off.'

Sadly for Beckham, by the time the finals came around, he was hampered by a metatarsal injury and not fully fit. Although he settled his score against Argentina by scoring the winner with a penalty when they met in the group stage, he was below his best as England lost to Brazil in the last eight.

It was a similar story at Euro 2004 in Portugal, where he saw one spot-kick saved in a group stage defeat by France and missed the target with another in a quarter-final shootout defeat by the hosts.

He defied illness and dehydration to become the first England player to score at three World Cups when his free-kick saw off Ecuador in the last-16 in 2006 but that tournament would end in tears too.

Beckham limped out of the last-eight tie with Portugal that again ended in agonising defeat on penalties then cried afterwards as he handed over the England captaincy

A star is born – Beckham celebrates his famous goal from the halfway line against Wimbledon.

After collecting a sixth Premier League winners' medal, Beckham was on his way out of Old Trafford.

in a media conference that was also the last of Eriksson's reign.

While he did return to the national team after initially being dropped by Steve McClaren, there was to be no final hurrah for his country. England failed to qualify for Euro 2008 and another injury meant his role at the 2010 World Cup was only as a non-playing member of Fabio Capello's support staff.

He had rather more success in his later years at club level, although he did not last much longer at Manchester United either.

'Posh and Becks' had tied the knot in 1999 and became the most famous married couple in the land. That, combined with Beckham's interest in fashion and finding new haircuts, seemed to irk Ferguson but they maintained an uneasy truce until things fully broke down at the start of 2003.

After a 2–0 defeat against Arsenal where Ferguson blamed Beckham for both goals, the player argued back. As the story goes, Ferguson swung a leg at a pile of clothes on the floor, connected with a stray boot and sent it flying towards Beckham's face in what was described as a 'freak accident'. The cut only required butterfly stitches, just above the eye, but more serious damage was done to their relationship.

By the summer, after collecting a sixth Premier League winners' medal, Beckham was on his way out of Old Trafford to join Cristiano Ronaldo, Zinedine Zidane and Luis Figo in a star-studded Real Madrid squad known as 'Galacticos'.

During his time in Spain he helped Real win La Liga and the Spanish Super Cup before moving to the United States with LA Galaxy in 2007, at the age of 31. He won the Major League Soccer (MLS) title twice but his real success was in boosting the global profile of the league, and he even increased his own celebrity too.

Beckham was loaned to AC Milan during the MLS off-season in 2009 and 2010 before a permanent move to France for a short spell with Paris St-Germain in 2013. He played his final professional game at the age of 38, having just helped PSG win the Ligue 1 title.

Beckham arrives for training with a plaster over his left eye after his clash with Sir Alex Ferguson in 2003.

'If you'd told me as a young boy I would have played for and won trophies with my boyhood club Manchester United, proudly captained and played for my country over 100 times and lined up for some of the biggest clubs in the world, I would have told you it was a fantasy,' he said after announcing his retirement. 'I'm fortunate to have realised those dreams.'

Since he stopped playing, Beckham has spent more time working as an ambassador with UNICEF, with whom he first took up a role in 2005, the same year he played a pivotal part in London's successful bid for the 2012 Olympics.

In 2014 he exercised an option to own an MLS franchise, which had been part of the deal offered to him when he joined LA Galaxy. The team he helped set up, Inter Miami, played their first games in 2020 and in echoes of his own move, signed World Cup winner Lionel Messi in 2023 with the aim of growing the game further in America.

John Barnes terrified opposition defences when he played for Liverpool and was always expected to do the same when he was wearing an England shirt.

7

John Barnes

Born	7 November 1963
Place of birth	Kingston, Jamaica
Position	Midfielder

John Barnes played 79 games for England between 1983 and 1995, scoring 11 goals, and won two English league titles, two FA Cups and a League Cup with Liverpool, where he played between 1987 and 1997. His former Reds team-mate Peter Beardsley described him as 'the best player I ever played with, bar none. For three or four years at the end of the 1980s, John was possibly the best player in the world.'

John Barnes was not the first Black footballer to play for England, but he was this country's first Black footballer to become a bona fide superstar.

At his absolute peak in the late 1980s he destroyed First Division defences on a regular basis but was denied the chance to do the same in continental club competition by the European ban that Liverpool served between 1985 and 1991 following the Heysel Stadium disaster.

For different reasons, he could never fully realise his talents on the global stage either. Former England manager Bobby Robson, who handed Barnes his first 58 caps between 1983 and 1990, called him 'the great enigma of international football' but that should not stop him from being remembered as one of the all-time greats.

Initially a tricky and fleet-footed goalscoring winger, his game evolved when he lost his electric pace through serious injury and he became a highly effective deep-lying playmaker, with his skill and intelligence allowing him to continue to impact games.

His brilliance brought its own issues. Because of the phenomenal start he made at international level, and his scintillating club form over many seasons, high expectations followed him for the rest of his England career.

He was not alone there, or with his struggles to cope with the more rigid structures of an international team compared to when he was playing for an elite club team built around his strengths, but on top of that Barnes also had to deal with the prejudices that existed against Black players of his day when it came to the public's perception of him.

His Jamaican heritage was often brought up when his inconsistent displays for England were compared to his breathtaking form for Liverpool and, as he explored in his 1999 autobiography, it was also part of what he described as 'the wider notion that John Barnes is too laid back.'

There were many other occasions when he was on the receiving end of racist abuse which was far more blatant and direct, and unfortunately it included the moment that he announced his arrival in an England shirt, his memorable solo goal against Brazil in Rio in June 1984.

Let's start with the goal itself, though. England have scored more than 2,300 times in close to 1,100 official matches since their first international match in 1872 but this is arguably the best of the lot, set in probably the most iconic stadium ever built.

Barnes's effort stands out from other spectacular individual efforts, like Paul Gascoigne's 1996 volley against Scotland or Jude Bellingham's overhead kick against Slovakia in 2024, for the same reason it is unusual compared to most of England's other great goals – namely that it does not involve the ball being smashed into the net.

It came at an unlikely time too. England were only heading to South America on a summer tour because they had failed miserably to qualify for the 1984 European Championship, and a young and inexperienced team had departed on the back of depressing defeats to France, Wales and the Soviet Union.

Few gave them a chance against Brazil, who had illuminated the 1982 World Cup and were viewed as magicians and masters even if many of their stars were missing for this match. They had only lost three

Barnes playing against the United States at Wembley in 1994.

times at the Maracanã Stadium in their history, but England would end up clinching a famous victory, inspired by Barnes's genius with a goal that came out of nothing.

There seems little danger when he picks up the ball on the left flank a minute from half-time, controlling a Mark Hateley knockdown with his chest just inside the Brazil half – these were the days when England preferred a target-man to a playmaker in the number 10 role.

But then Barnes starts running, and does not stop, cutting inside and going past man after man at high speed as if they are not there, gliding past three defenders then into the area with one last body swerve into space.

Once he is inside the box he dances past two more Brazilians before wrong footing goalkeeper Roberto Costa and casually slotting the ball into the net from the edge of the six-yard box as if he is playing 5-a-side football against his friends.

It all happens in the space of seven glorious seconds, and there has not been an England goal like it before or since. 'I don't remember much about it and in fact even when I do see it on TV again, it is like having an out-of-body experience,' Barnes would later say.

The vast and at one-time magnificent Maracanã Stadium was at that stage semi-derelict and, despite a crowd of 56,000, was less than a third full, but everyone was off their seat to salute him – including the Brazil fans.

'This was a goal of such brilliance that even their own favourite Pelé would have been proud of it,' read *The Daily Telegraph*'s report. Repeated viewings of the grainy footage on YouTube are well worthwhile now but, unfortunately for Barnes, who went on to set up a second goal for Hateley, that was what people demanded at the time too.

'Barnes had to live with that goal from then on as everyone expected him to repeat it every time he pulled on an England

Barnes made his name at Watford after being recommended to the Hornets by a taxi driver.

shirt, and they were disappointed when he didn't,' Robson wrote in his 1990 book *Against All Odds*.

For Barnes, who was still only 20, it was the moment that his entire international career would always be judged on. He would later admit that he tried too hard to replicate that moment whenever he played for England, attempting too many mazy dribbles and losing the ball.

'Events in the Maracanã did not change me but they did change the English public's attitude towards me,' Barnes said at the end of his career. 'They expected me to do that dribble again and again and again.

'When I passed, fans wondered why I wasn't dribbling. If I didn't score, fans wondered why. I could hear them moaning "why isn't John Barnes taking on defenders like he did against Brazil?"'

There were more unsavoury reactions to his goal later on the same tour, which also saw England play Uruguay and Chile.

On the team's flight from Montevideo to Santiago, a small group of England fans – or, more accurately, National Front activists posing as supporters – were on the same plane and shouted racist abuse down the plane aisle at the three Black players in the England squad – Barnes, Viv Anderson and Mark Chamberlain.

Sadly, this was the kind of treatment Barnes and other Black players in England were used to in the 1980s, when they were still something of a rarity in the national team.

When Anderson became the first Black footballer to play for England men's senior team in 1978, *The Observer* newspaper used the headline 'The black revolution in English football isn't coming. It is here' but it took time for that to be the case, and Anderson was the only black or mixed-race player in their 22-man squad for the 1980 European Championship and the 1982 World Cup.

More than 100 Black men have played for England since, and at Euro 2024, the Three Lions had 13 players with Black heritage in their 26-man squad, but Barnes was one of the pioneers, becoming only the seventh Black England player when he replaced Watford team-mate Luther Blissett (the fifth) in the second half of a 0–0 draw with Northern Ireland at Windsor Park on 28 May 1983.

Ethnicity should not be important when you consider the

merits of any player or person but unfortunately it is relevant here. Barnes's background affected how he was regarded throughout his career and the criticism he received, something he wrote about in his 2021 book *The Uncomfortable Truth About Racism* which addressed how deep rooted the problem is in society, not just football.

Events that same year showed the issue had not gone away, four decades on. When Jadon Sancho, Marcus Rashford and Bukayo Saka missed or had their penalties saved as England lost to Italy in the shootout that decided the final of Euro 2020 – which was delayed by a year because of the coronavirus – all three received vicious racist abuse on social media.

For Barnes, the biggest difference was that he frequently had to put up with that kind of treatment to his face, even when he was playing.

He was born in Jamaica, the son of a senior officer in the army, and moved to England aged 12 when his father was sent to London on a diplomatic posting.

When his family returned to Jamaica four years later, Barnes was planning to go back too. He had been offered a football scholarship with Washington University in the United States, but instead his life and career quickly went in a very different direction.

A taxi driver saw Barnes playing for Middlesex League side Sudbury Court and recommended him to a scout at Watford. After going to train with the Hornets in the summer of 1981, he was offered a contract, with Sudbury receiving a set of kits in return.

From there, things progressed quickly. Barnes scored from 25 yards after 30 seconds of his first appearance in Watford's reserves and, within weeks, he was in their first team and playing in the old Second Division at the age of 17 – he made his debut against Oldham on 5 September 1981.

Barnes scored 13 goals as Watford won promotion that season, the culmination of a remarkable rise under chairman Elton John and manager Graham Taylor that saw them go from Division Four to Division One in the space of five years, and they would go on to finish runners-up to Liverpool in 1982–83, their first ever campaign in the top flight.

The fairytale continued the following season when they reached the 1984 FA Cup final and even a defeat to Everton could not take the shine off the day for Barnes.

'For Watford to reach an FA Cup final was so special,' he told *FourFourTwo* in 2017. 'I'd played at Wembley for England by then, but nothing could prepare me for an FA Cup final. The atmosphere was incredible. I remember Elton coming into our dressing room, it was such a proud day for him especially. I had an early chance, but that Everton team was very hard to beat.'

While it would be wrong to suggest that Barnes's progress stagnated after that, because his form for Watford remained impressive, leading to interest from Arsenal, Tottenham and Manchester United, his career only truly ignited when he joined Liverpool for £900,000 in June 1987 and formed a devastating attacking combination with Peter Beardsley and John Aldridge.

Barnes celebrates the first of his two goals in Liverpool's 4–0 win over QPR in October 1987, remembered as one of their finest performances in that season's title win.

Barnes was in dazzling form to help the Reds win the title in his first year at Anfield, and also scooped the Professional Footballers' Association and Football Writers' Player of the Year awards, but unfortunately the racists were never far away.

This was the same season he was pictured backheeling a banana off the pitch at Goodison Park after it had been flung at him by an Everton fan during an FA Cup tie. It is one of the most iconic photographs of the 1980s, but Barnes says it was nothing new to him – he had already been pelted with the fruit twice in the space of four days when Everton had visited Anfield in the League Cup and for a league game a few months earlier.

Barnes gets ready for Watford's 1984 FA Cup semi-final against Plymouth with the club's flamboyant chairman Elton John and team-mate Mo Johnston. Barnes set up George Reilly's winner to send the Hornets to Wembley.

'It was a different world for black people then, not just black players,' Barnes told the BBC when he was asked about the incident in 2020. 'That's what we have to understand. I don't know why even now why we are trying to separate football from the rest of the world as if it's a problem in football and nowhere else.

'Back then, the problem we had with that situation was when it was Liverpool versus Everton, the two top teams. I am backheeling a banana so it came to the fore in the front pages of the newspapers, but it had been going on for the past 10 years.

'I suppose it was a shock to some people but I had been experiencing that in my time at Watford in most games that we went to. It just wasn't highlighted because of the lack of media attention at the smaller clubs.'

As appalling as that abuse was, Barnes did not let it affect him. As well as shining for Liverpool, including his part in a stunning 5–0 win over Nottingham Forest that is still hailed as one of the finest team performances ever seen, he was superb as England clinched a statement 4–1 win over Yugoslavia in Belgrade on their way to topping their qualifying group for the 1988 European Championship.

It was a result that ensured they were among the favourites for the finals in West Germany, bringing hopes that he would bring his best form to those finals too.

Barnes's only previous appearance at a major tournament, at the 1986 World Cup in Mexico, had been belated, and extremely brief. Even now it remains a tantalising glimpse of what might have been for him and England too.

Robson had left him on the bench for the first four matches in Mexico, in the group stage and then against Paraguay in the last 16, but Barnes was summoned to action for the finale of England's infamous quarter-final against Diego Maradona's Argentina, coming on with just under 16 minutes to go and his side 2–0 down.

Barnes takes almost five minutes to get his first touch, a header under pressure that is deflected out of play, and another 90 seconds before he receives his first pass, from Steve Hodge, but his impact after collecting the ball on the left-hand corner of the Argentina area is instant. He surges past Ricardo Giusti to reach the by-line then stands up a perfectly weighted

England are out, with their fans wondering what might have been if Barnes had been given longer . . .

cross for Gary Lineker to head past Nery Pumpido from close range.

After an amazing amount of time-wasting by Argentina, Barnes finally has another chance to run at their defence with less than three minutes remaining. Again he leaves Giusti in his dust, and again he sends over an inviting cross for Lineker, who is poised to nod home from point-blank range at the back post, only for Julio Olarticoechea to somehow reach the ball first, from underneath him.

It bounces wide, leaving only a disbelieving Lineker in the back of the net and still working out how he has not equalised. England are out, with their fans wondering what might have been if Barnes had been given longer on the pitch.

Two years on, at the 1988 European Championship, with Barnes now a fixture in Robson's team rather than on the fringes, expectations were high that he would make up for lost time but, like his club-mate Beardsley, he appeared drained by Liverpool's long season and was a shadow of his usual self that summer. Barnes played the full 90 minutes in England's three group games, but they lost all of them.

More trophies followed at club level, with Barnes setting up Ian Rush to score the winner against Everton in the 1989 FA Cup final, but that triumph was overshadowed by the Hillsborough disaster when 97 people died at the Reds' semi-final against Nottingham Forest.

At the 1990 World Cup, Barnes was still in his prime and surely things would be different for him with England this time? Again, the build-up was promising – after scoring 22 goals to help Liverpool win another league title, he had excelled along with fellow-winger Chris Waddle in a vital 3–0 qualifying win over Poland.

In Italy, he was initially used as a strike partner for Lineker, but had a volleyed goal wrongly disallowed for offside against Belgium for what would have been the winner. Instead, David Platt was the hero for his spectacular and last-gasp effort, while Barnes limped off with a groin injury and although he started the quarter-final against Cameroon, he was not fully fit and came off at half-time.

That was his last involvement not just in that World Cup, but in any major finals and, while Paul Gascoigne and Platt set that tournament in Italy alight, Barnes's part in it is probably best remembered for his iconic rap in New Order's England song 'World in Motion'.

Although he was set to be named in Graham Taylor's squad for the 1992 European Championship, he tore his Achilles tendon in the final warm-up friendly against Finland. It was a serious injury, which would shape the way Barnes's

Barnes and Gary Lineker relax by the pool during the 1986 World Cup.

Barnes with his Watford team-mate Luther Blissett in 1987. They played together three times for England.

game evolved in the latter stages of his career. When he returned, six months later, his electric pace had gone and he could not hurt teams the way he once had.

'The player I was until 1992, the fast player on the left, creating chances, was gone,' he recalled in 2020. 'When I ruptured my Achilles tendon at 28, they didn't think I would play again. They didn't tell me that until I retired, and I saw the surgeon who did the operation and he said we didn't think you'd play again. I had to go into midfield and become a different type of player, so I was not the player I was.'

Barnes kept his England place, but the team was struggling under his old Watford manager Taylor, and the fans took their frustrations out on him. He was booed by a section of the Wembley crowd in 1993, during a lacklustre qualifying win over San Marino when he was far from the worst performer. His response was to curl home a wonderful free-kick against the Netherlands in England's next home game. It was a reminder of his immense talent, but it would be his final goal for his country.

Switched to a deeper, central role by Liverpool manager Roy Evans, he was surprisingly recalled by new national boss Terry Venables after being left out of his first three squads in 1994, but did not make the squad for Euro '96.

His final England appearance was against Colombia at Wembley in September 1995. This time it was a South American who stole the show, with visiting goalkeeper René Higuita keeping out a long-range shot from Barnes's Liverpool team-mate Jamie Redknapp with an unorthodox and spectacular forward flip that became known as the 'Scorpion Kick'.

Barnes came on for Redknapp for the last 16 minutes of the game, the same amount of time he had been given in the 1986 World Cup, a final reminder of the force he could have been for England.

At club level, he left Liverpool for Newcastle in 1997 after 108 goals in 407 appearances for the Reds. He ended his playing career with Charlton in 1999 and had short spells in management with Celtic, Jamaica and Tranmere Rovers.

As well as being an author, Barnes has also worked as a Premier League pundit in Malaysia, Abu Dhabi and South Africa and is now back at Anfield as an official ambassador.

Paul Gascoigne's rise to stardom began at Newcastle when he helped the Magpies win the 1985 FA Youth Cup.

Paul Gascoigne

Born	27 May 1967
Place of birth	Gateshead, Tyne and Wear
Position	Midfielder

Paul Gascoigne won 57 caps for England between 1988 and 1998 and scored 10 goals for his country. Injury and controversy dogged his career but tears at Italia 90 made him a national hero and his spectacular volley against Scotland at Euro '96 provided another of English football's most memorable moments.

While the other players mentioned in this book undoubtedly made the absolute maximum of their ability, Paul Gascoigne's critics will always ask what he could have achieved had he not possessed the inclination for self-destruction that hampered him during his playing days and which has haunted him since he hung up his boots.

Gascoigne, known universally by his nickname Gazza, is probably the most naturally gifted of any player in England's long footballing history when it comes to his instinctive individual skill, and will forever be remembered as a fragile and flawed genius or unfulfilled talent, yet this madcap and maverick midfielder was still the star of England's two stand-out campaigns in the 55 years between their World Cup win in 1966 and their next appearance in a major final, at the European Championship in 2021.

His unique combination of exuberance and vulnerability that he showed at the 1990 World Cup won him a place in the nation's hearts that he did not lose even when his unforgivable abusive behaviour towards his former wife Sheryl became public knowledge.

> 'It's about 35 years since I've seen a kid as good as this lad is, he's got everything.'
> – *Jack Charlton*

Gascoigne's trademark pranks did not seem so harmless after that, and the dark side of his character cannot and should not be ignored, but his popularity endured. Sadly, the battle with his demons has often overwhelmed him with mental health problems in recent years, and he has spoken openly about how alcoholism has affected his professional and personal life, but it was actually always present, in the shape of eating disorders and addiction to prescription drugs, even when he was producing and providing pure joy with his performances on the pitch.

Trauma of some kind seems ever-present in Gascoigne's life and perhaps can be traced back to the age of 10, when he witnessed the death of the younger brother of a friend in a traffic accident and, soon afterwards, developed twitches and tics.

Back then, however, he always had football too. Scouts began to notice him from the age of 12, when he was playing for Redheugh Boys' Club Under-14s. Middlesbrough and Ipswich were the first to approach his parents to offer him a trial, then Southampton, but he waited for an offer from his beloved Newcastle – which finally came when he was taken on as a schoolboy in the summer of 1980.

Gascoigne became a ball-boy at St James' Park and was also Kevin Keegan's boot-boy when he joined the club two years later – famously losing half of his hero's footwear when he took it to school to show his friends – before signing as an apprentice on his 16th birthday.

He made his first-team debut aged 17 against Queens Park Rangers in April 1985 when he was still living with his parents in Dunston, on the south banks of the Tyne, and immediately afterwards helped the youth team win the prestigious FA Youth Cup, scoring twice as captain to seal victory in a 4–1 win over Watford in the second leg of the final.

On the coach journey home from Vicarage Road, Newcastle manager and World Cup winner Jack Charlton told Gascoigne he was going to offer him a two-year professional contract. Charlton, who would resign before the start of the following season, had seen something special and said at the time 'I think it's about 35 years since I've seen a kid as good as this lad is, he's got everything. Everything.'

Plenty of young players have been talked up like that before and since, but Gascoigne was different in that he lived up to that potential. Although he struggled with his weight as a teenager – he was once pelted with Mars Bars by Middlesbrough fans when he went to take a corner – some fine displays for Newcastle saw him win a call-up by the England Under-21 squad and he was named the Professional Footballers' Association Young Player of the Year in 1988.

By now he was 21 and Britain's brightest young talent. Liverpool, the league champions, were interested and held informal talks but Manchester United were the first to make a firm offer that summer. Gascoigne told their manager Sir Alex Ferguson the deal would be done – but then changed his mind and, while Ferguson was on holiday in Malta, moved to Terry Venables' Tottenham for a British record fee of £2 m instead.

'I don't regret not playing for United but at the same time I have thought about that decision

Gascoigne joined Middlesbrough in March 1998 and made his debut as a substitute in the League Cup final.

If only . . . Gascoigne just fails to connect with Alan Shearer's cross during golden goal extra-time of England's Euro '96 semi-final defeat by Germany.

a lot,' Gascoigne told *FourFourTwo* magazine in 2004. 'I told Sir Alex I was signing for United and that he should go away and enjoy his summer holiday.

'I drove to Old Trafford to put pen to paper, but I kept on driving and eventually joined Tottenham. I was only young and looked to others for guidance. I had a great relationship with Chris Waddle, a Newcastle player with me who had moved to Spurs, and he told me to come and join him because he adored it down there.

'Then Terry called me up and that impressed me. He promised he would get me in the England squad in three months, and it only took two. I enjoyed my time at Spurs but I do look back and wonder what my life would have been like if I'd signed for United.'

Many others have pondered what might have happened had Ferguson, a famous disciplinarian, become the authority figure in Gascoigne's chaotic life. He still prospered at Spurs, but his immaturity meant England manager Bobby Robson was initially reluctant to trust him fully.

After that first senior call-up saw him make his full England debut as a late substitute in a 1–0 friendly win against Denmark in

September 1988, more landmarks followed. He scored his first international goal in a 5–0 win over Albania in a World Cup qualifier in April 1989 and made his first start for his country against Chile a month later.

Still, doubts remained about whether he would make the England squad for the 1990 World Cup as they prepared for a friendly against Czechoslovakia at Wembley on 25 April, only 45 days before the start of the tournament.

Robson, who famously called Gascoigne 'daft as a brush' before the game, was worried that he was unable to follow his tactical instructions and questioned him publicly in a media conference when he was asked who he would pick to play alongside Bryan Robson in midfield.

'The man who plays with Robson has to have brains and discipline,' Bobby said. 'He has to be able to work out when to go and when to stay, when to take chances. I am not saying Gascoigne hasn't got a brain, but he still has to learn when to use it.'

That left Gascoigne 'terrified' that he would not make Robson's 22-man squad for Italy but he responded with a performance that made him virtually impossible to leave out.

England won 4–2 and Gascoigne recalled how 'everything I did came off. I walked off the pitch pretty sure I'd be in the squad. To play a faultless game, to score, to set up two goals for Steve Bull and to get the press boys screaming for me to play made it a great night.'

Gascoigne did indeed make the plane – despite forgetting to bring his passport to the airport – and, before a ball was kicked, he celebrated his 23rd birthday in Italy by having a cake planted into his face by his old friend Waddle as the squad relaxed by the pool.

When the serious business began, Gascoigne was in the starting XI but initially he could not make an impression as England toiled to draws with the Republic of Ireland and the Netherlands in their first two matches.

His World Cup only got going in England's final group game against Egypt when he set up Mark Wright's winner, and Gascoigne did not look back. He repeated the trick in the last-16 against Belgium, winning a last-gasp free-kick with a driving run forward and then delivering the ball for David Platt to swivel and smash home.

Another superb performance, and a pass that led to a crucial Gary Lineker penalty, followed in the quarter-final win over Cameroon, and despite more off-field antics – he played tennis for hours in the blazing sun with tourists after being ordered to rest, shoved Lineker's wife off a yacht and was also the ringleader in the hotel high-jinks that saw Bryan Robson return home with a badly-cut foot – had emerged as one of the stars of the tournament by the time England faced West Germany in the semi-final.

This was English football's biggest moment since 1966, not that Gascoigne seemed to notice from the way he went about his battle with opposite number Lothar Matthaus, considered the best midfielder in the world. 'He just went out and played like it was a Sunday morning pub game with his mates,' remembered Waddle.

Ultimately Germany would prevail on penalties but the game itself is as famous for Gascoigne's tears as the end result. He is seen welling up after being booked for a lunge on Thomas Berthold in the first half of extra-time, and knows the yellow card will rule him out of the final if England get there. As he fights his emotions, Gary Lineker is seen signalling to the bench that they need to keep an eye on him.

'When I got booked I just wanted the ground to open up, you know,' Gascoigne said later. 'It's the worst feeling I've ever had in soccer.'

That display of emotion only made the public love him more. After that heartbreak, the England squad still returned home to a heroes' welcome, with 'Gazzamania' at full tilt. As well as signing dozens of lucrative endorsement deals, he won the BBC's Sports Personality of the Year for 1990, and also appeared on *Top of the Pops* to sing 'Fog on the Tyne'.

His overall impact was arguably even greater than that. Football, in a dark place in England for much of the previous decade because of widespread hooliganism that had seen crowds dip dramatically, exploded in popularity again on the back of that World Cup. It also seemed to suddenly have a new, diverse and family-friendly audience. Much of it could be put down to Gascoigne.

There was, of course, a flip side to this new-found fame and intense media attention. While the hype around Gascoigne seemed to inspire him to new heights on the pitch too, particularly in the

FA Cup when he hit six goals on Tottenham's run to the 1991 final, his uncontrollable enthusiasm also led to a serious injury that almost derailed his career for good.

Watch highlights of those FA Cup games back now and Gascoigne is at his hyperactive, hypnotising best, using his extraordinary upper-body strength to run straight through defenders and finding the net. The best goal of the lot, though, is the brilliant long-range free-kick he fired past Arsenal at Wembley in the semi-finals.

'I remember Lineker coming up to me, and he just told me to hit it,' Gascoigne told the BBC in 1995. 'It was just after a hernia operation so it was a bit iffy, but I just give it everything and it flew in the back of the net. David Seaman got a little hand to it, but you know he should have just left it.'

The final against Nottingham Forest was just as dramatic, but for all the wrong reasons. A manic Gascoigne is lucky to stay on the pitch after a chest-high tackle on Garry Parker after only two minutes,

Gascoigne celebrated his 23rd birthday in typical style during the 1990 World Cup.

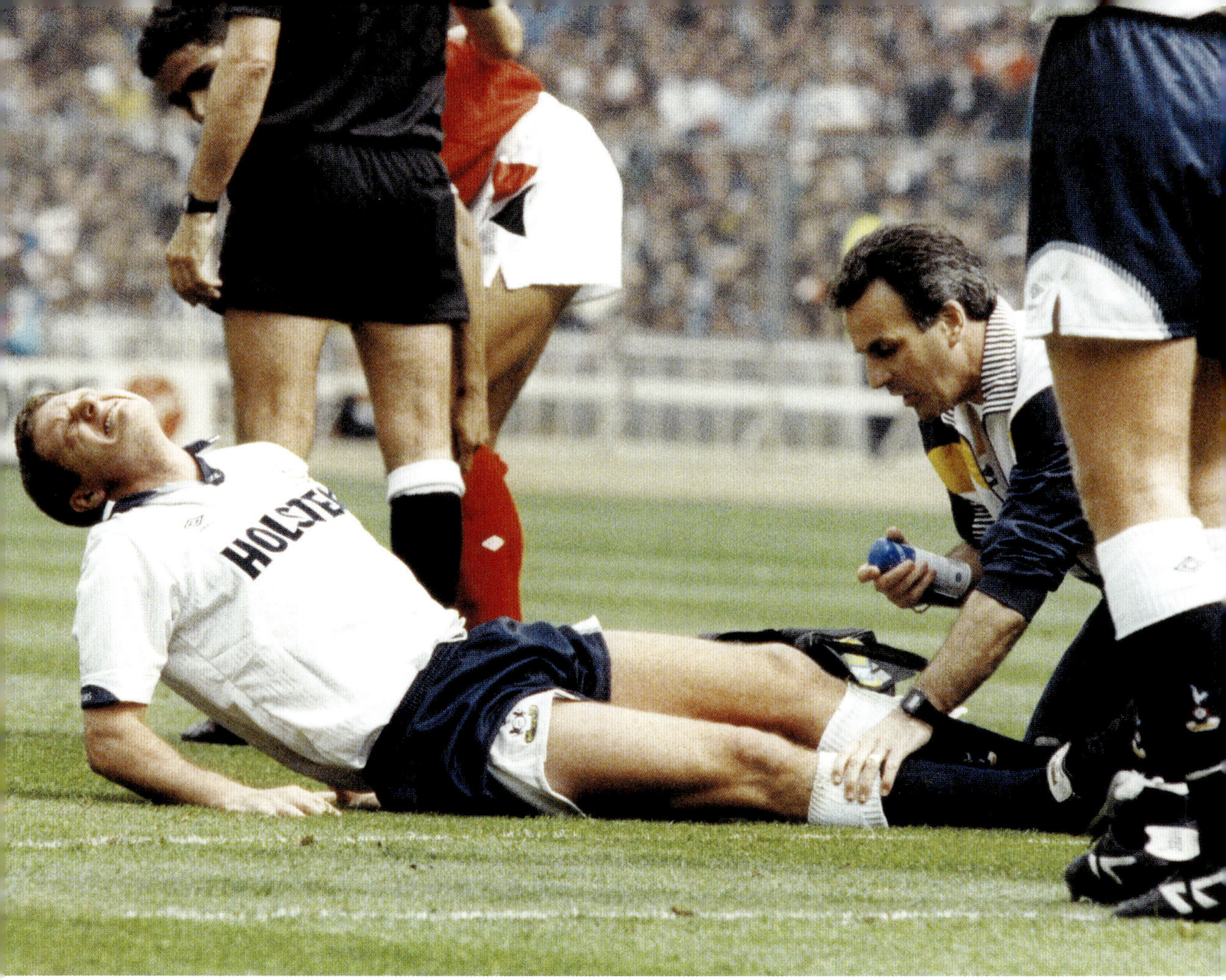

Gascoigne receives treatment on his injured knee after his infamous challenge on Nottingham Forest's Gary Charles in the 1991 FA Cup final.

but does not learn his lesson and soon follows that up with another wild lunge on Gary Charles.

'Charles was coming down the right,' Gascoigne told Radio 5 Live in 2011. 'His touch brought him inside and I was off balance. I tried to get a good challenge on him to let him know he was in a game.'

Instead, that challenge was disastrous. It ruptured a cruciate ligament in Gascoigne's right knee and sidelined him for over a year. The fact Spurs went on to win the FA Cup was irrelevant as Gascoigne attempted to save his career and salvage a multi-million pound transfer to Lazio.

An incident a few months later at a Tyneside nightclub, where he suffered another knee injury, this time a fractured kneecap, delayed his comeback further and, although Gascoigne eventually returned to fitness and moved to Italy – he made his Lazio debut against Genoa on 27 September 1992 and remains hugely popular in Rome – he showed only fleeting glimpses of his brilliance during his three years in Serie A.

He would play only 47 games for Lazio and completed 90 minutes in only 17 of them. That time of his career saw more indiscipline and injuries than anything else, and he was unable to find his best form to save England's doomed bid to reach the 1994 World Cup.

Gascoigne seemed happier when he returned to Britain to play for Glasgow Rangers in 1995 and the following summer, with his old Spurs boss Venables installed as the Three Lions coach, Euro '96 gave him the stage he craved to be an international star again.

Of course, with Gascoigne involved, there was controversy too. The England squad was criticised even before the European Championship started when they went on a heavy drinking session on a pre-tournament trip to Hong Kong, and there was a siege mentality in their camp because of the negative media coverage.

A lot of it was aimed at Gascoigne, who was one of those pictured drunk in the papers, and more vitriol followed when he struggled and was substituted as England began with a disappointing draw against Switzerland. Sporting a new haircut, he was accused of being a bleached-blonde passenger, past his pomp and unable to run midfield the same way he could in his physical prime.

His response in England's next match, against Scotland, was to score one of the most spectacular goals ever seen by anyone in an England shirt, sealing a 2–0 victory by flicking the ball over Colin Hendry and smashing a first-time strike into the net, and marked it with a memorable celebration mimicking the 'Dentist's Chair' drinking game he had been castigated for participating in a few weeks earlier.

'Sensational. That was vintage Gascoigne,' was Venables' verdict afterwards. England followed that by demolishing the Netherlands 4–1, with Gascoigne playing another inspirational role, and then edged past Spain on penalties in the quarter-finals to set up another clash with Germany in the last four. Again, it was a desperately close and tense affair, and again it would end in desolation.

For Gascoigne and England, it came so close to being a different story. This time extra-time could be settled by a golden goal – whoever scored first, won.

Darren Anderton was the first player to go close when he hit the post and then, for a split second, it appears Gascoigne would be the man to settle it.

Teddy Sheringham plays a high ball over to Alan Shearer on the right of the area and he volleys the ball across goal towards Gascoigne, who is running in at the back post.

'Every time I watch it, I still think he is going to score,' Paul Ince told the BBC in 2022.

Unfortunately, although Gascoigne has read the cross, he checks his run slightly, expecting Germany keeper Andreas Köpke to get a touch on the ball. He doesn't, so Gascoigne arrives slightly too late. He hurls himself forward in desperation but his out-stretched left boot is millimetres away from making contact.

That is how close England got to reaching the final. Instead, they lost in another shootout. Gascoigne's reaction was to run to his hotel room and 'have a good cry', but not before pouring a large tub of ketchup over team-mate Robbie Fowler.

He did not know it at the time, but that defeat was Gascoigne's last involvement in a major tournament. He was a regular in the next qualification campaign under Glenn Hoddle and played all three games when England won Le Tournoi in 1997, a four-nation tournament held in France as a warm-up for the World Cup they were hosting the following year, but he did not make it back across the Channel for the real thing.

Instead, his decade-long international career was ended when he found out on the eve of the 1998 World Cup that he was not in the final squad. He trashed the hotel room in La Manga where he was given the news.

Gascoigne had returned to play in England with Middlesbrough to play under his old midfield partner Bryan Robson earlier that year and was still only 31, but the years of chaos and improper refuelling – as another former national manager Graham Taylor once put it – had caught up with him.

A furious Hoddle had seen pictures of Gascoigne out on a pub-crawl and eating a late-night kebab in the week before they headed for Spain and had told him he was worried about his condition. He had actually made his mind up before they left London.

'After all I had seen of him physically and mentally, I knew deep down he had run out

Gascoigne's goal against Scotland at Euro '96 is remembered as one of England's greatest ever, and so is the way he celebrated it.

Gascoigne's tears during the 1990 World Cup semi-final won him a place in the nation's hearts.

of time,' Hoddle wrote in his World Cup diary. 'At the airport, it kept coming to me that I couldn't take Gazza to France.'

Gascoigne was short of full fitness but had started England's final warm-up game against Belgium and still expected to be included in the final 22. He reacted angrily when he was told otherwise and had to be restrained by Ince and David Seaman, and was escorted out after giving Hoddle an earful, overturning a table and smashing a vase.

'I'm the next person in after Gazza,' his old Boro team-mate Paul Merson recalled in 2022. 'I walk in and Glenn is sitting at the other end of the room, and you'd think he had seen a ghost. The room was everywhere – chairs, lampshade – everything was wrecked. Forget about the football, Paul was in a bad way – he was ill.'

There was real concern for Gascoigne from his team-mates. 'I genuinely feared for him and his life, because of the way he was,' Darren Anderton told *The Daily Telegraph* when the incident was revisited years later. 'The boys were worried for him. What would he do without football, without going to a World Cup? The

It was the end for Gascoigne and England, no matter who was in charge.

shock of it would have killed him. Thankfully that didn't happen.'

It was the end for Gascoigne and England, no matter who was in charge or how hard he tried.

Even being reunited with his old Rangers manager and mentor Walter Smith when he moved to Everton in 2000 could not provide the spark for a sustained spell of his old form.

While some sporadic signs of his ability led to occasional suggestions by him and others that he could return to the England fold, an international recall never seemed a serious prospect as his 30s progressed.

After leaving Everton in 2002, brief stints with Burnley, Chinese B-League side Gansu Tianma, Wolves, where he was not offered a contract, and Boston United, where he was player-coach, were the final stops of a playing career that slowly faded before finishing for good in 2004, while a six-week spell in charge of Conference North side Kettering Town in 2005 – when he claimed the club's owner had tried to pick the team – was the only time he tried management.

His football career was combustible enough but his physical and mental problems seem to have accelerated since the end of his direct involvement in the game, not helped by the treatment he continued to receive as a target of the tabloid press.

In 1995, he had told the BBC his ambition was just to try to be happy in life, but contentment continued to elude him, decades on.

Out of any England player who failed to secure a major international prize, and there are hundreds of them, it is easier to imagine alternative, more successful, timelines for Gascoigne than anyone else – if he had joined United, not been booked in 1990 or reached that cross in 1996 – but it would be wrong to look back at what he achieved and consider it a disappointment, because he still gave England fans so much joy.

Perhaps it is in his absolute prime, at Italia 90, where we should remember him. As he wrote in his memoirs, he wished that tournament would never end.

Geoff Hurst led the line for West Ham and England during a golden period for his club and country.

9

GEOFF HURST

Born	8 December 1941
Place of birth	Ashton-under-Lyne, Lancashire
Position	Centre-forward

Geoff Hurst scored 24 goals in 49 appearances for England between 1966 and 1972 and was also prolific at club level, where he managed 242 goals in 500 appearances during his 15 years at West Ham, but he is synonymous with just one of those games, the 1966 World Cup final, after famously being selected over Jimmy Greaves, who had begun the tournament as first-choice.

'And here comes Hurst! He's got . . . some people are on the pitch, they think it is all over . . . it is now . . . it's four.'

Kenneth Wolstenholme's description of the final moments of the 1966 World Cup final forms arguably the most famous piece of football commentary there has ever been, but it is sometimes misquoted because he re-recorded it, using slightly different wording, for use in New Order's 1990 England World Cup song, 'World in Motion'.

Whichever version you know best, hearing it again still perfectly captures the sense of history in the making as Geoff Hurst achieves sporting immortality, putting the seal on England's triumph by making the final score 4–2 and becoming the first man to score a hat-trick in a World Cup final.

Those three very different goals – one deliberate header, one instinctive right-foot shot on the turn and another rasping strike with his left on the run – are what have put him in the pantheon of greats, and it is a personal landmark that still stands. Although France's Kylian Mbappé repeated the feat

56 years later, he was on the losing side against Argentina in the final in Qatar in 2022. Hurst is still the only player to achieve it, and win, in what was just his eighth appearance for his country.

He did not quite come from nowhere to take his place in footballing folklore but one of the hallmarks of any great centre-forward is being in the right place at the right time and Hurst certainly managed that in 1966, continuing a trait that shaped his entire career.

Hurst was not a striker when he started out, and football was not even his strongest sport. He had been more successful playing cricket as a schoolboy in Chelmsford, Essex, and was only offered a trial by West Ham when he was 15 because, without Hurst's knowledge, a friend of his father's had written to Arsenal and the Hammers suggesting they take a look at him.

Back then, he was a midfielder, or wing-half using the parlance of the day. West Ham had to wait to see what he could do – Hurst missed his first trial at the club after getting lost on the London Underground – but when they did see him play they were impressed and, by the time Arsenal got round to replying and invited him over a few weeks later, he was already on the Hammers' books.

When Hurst left school aged 16 in 1957, West Ham wanted to keep him and offered him an apprenticeship but he found playing opportunities limited, not helped by the fact he was competing for a place in the team with a certain Bobby Moore, who similarly was yet to move back into defence and find his own niche.

Hurst, who had continued playing cricket each summer and was good enough to play regularly as a wicketkeeper at county level for Essex's second team, had a decision to make. He was contemplating a permanent switch to the summer sport when Ron Greenwood arrived as Hammers coach in 1961.

Hurst always credits Greenwood as being the man who changed his life, starting with the moment he suggested he try a different playing position after deciding his sturdy physique, including a pair of famously thick thighs, would be better suited to leading the forward line.

'I remember it very clearly,' Hurst told the BBC's *Match of Their Day* programme in 1999. 'It was 1962, only four years before the

Hurst holds aloft the Jules Rimet Trophy at Wembley, joined by team-mates Nobby Stiles, Bobby Moore, Martin Peters and Roger Hunt.

World Cup final, and I was playing more cricket than football. I played that summer for Essex's first team against Lancashire, when the West Ham team went across to Africa, so I wasn't involved at that stage.

'Then the season started and I was playing in midfield, and I played a game on the Saturday, against Shrewsbury in the reserves. I wasn't quite fit, because I was still playing cricket as well, and struggled a bit.

'On the Monday morning, all the players were at the training ground and Ron came up to me and asked if I had played on Saturday. I said yes but explained that I didn't play well. Ron said to forget about that and asked me if I wanted to have a go up front against Liverpool that night.'

And so it began for Geoff Hurst, striker. The 20-year-old played in attack for the first time with Johnny Byrne in a 1–0 win over the Merseysiders in the old Division One on 3 September 1962 and stayed there for the rest of the season, playing 27 league games and scoring 13 goals.

Hurst says the advice of Greenwood helped him learn how to become a centre-forward but his transformation also owed much to the work he put in on the training ground, giving him

Hurst lets fly with his thunderbolt finish to complete his hat-trick in the World Cup final.

nous to go with his mobility and skill. While he performed the role of an old-fashioned target-man, the term did not do him justice and there is a strong argument that he reinvented the role.

His pace and power made him a handful for defences, and he became adept at dragging defenders out of position to make space for others. On top of that, his ability to hold up the ball and bring others into the game added another dimension to his play, particularly when he chested long high passes down and shielded the ball from the opposition.

He became known for the ferocity of his finishing, usually with his cheeks blowing when he kicked the ball – Hammers fans nicknamed him 'Puffer' because of that habit – and the goals kept flowing over the next four seasons, including one at Wembley when West Ham beat

While he performed the role of an old-fashioned target-man, the term did not do him justice . . .

Preston to win the FA Cup in 1964. He also led their attack as they won the European Cup Winners' Cup the following season.

Individual recognition arrived too, with four England Under-23 caps, but Hurst says he was still surprised when he got his first senior call-up for his country, which came only months before the 1966 World Cup began.

He was selected in the squad to face Poland at Goodison Park in January of that year but did not play. Instead his debut came against who else but West Germany at Wembley on 23 February. England won that game too, 1–0 thanks to a Nobby Stiles goal.

The race for a place in the World Cup team was on, and Hurst initially did enough to impress the manager, Alf Ramsey. He started England's next two games, scoring his first international goal in a thrilling 4–3 win over Scotland at Hampden Park in April and then playing his part in an impressive attacking performance in their final home game before the tournament, a 2–0 win over Yugoslavia at Wembley in May.

When the squad for the finals was announced at the start of June, Hurst was given the number 10 shirt which indicated he would partner Jimmy Greaves, who at that time was arguably the greatest goalscorer in the world and came into the tournament with an astonishing strike-rate of 43 goals in 51 internationals. Greaves would wear number eight, and the other striker in the squad, Roger Hunt, was number 21. The number nine shirt, traditionally worn by a centre-forward, went to Bobby Charlton.

So far, so good . . . but something changed Ramsey's mind during England's next warm-up matches. Hurst struggled to make an impact against Finland and Denmark, while in between those games, Greaves and Hunt prospered together in a 6–1 win over Norway.

'I thought the final pre-tournament match, against Poland in Chorzow, would give the critical clue to Alf's intentions,' Hurst wrote in his 2001 autobiography. 'This game was just six days before the World Cup kicked off. When Alf chose Jimmy and Roger as his front two I knew I wouldn't be in

> 'The best England goal I ever saw in my time with the squad.'
> *– Bobby Charlton*

the starting line-up for the first World Cup game against Uruguay.'

Hurst was right, and he would be a spectator for the entire group stage. Greaves and Hunt also started together against Mexico and France and even though Greaves failed to score in any of those three matches, they surely would have continued as the first-choice pairing for the remainder of the tournament but for the badly-gashed shin that Greaves sustained against the French, which ruled him out of the clash with Argentina in the last 16.

This was Hurst's big opportunity and, typically, he took it, scoring a brilliant winner. 'I was relaxed and I was ready,' he remembered years later, with his comfort about coming into the team bolstered by having his friends and West Ham team-mates, Moore and Martin Peters, lining up with him.

While many tempers boiled over in a famously bad-tempered match, Hurst was only focused on finding the net. Chances were hard to come by, though, even when Argentina were reduced to 10 men, until 13 minutes from time when Peters and Hurst combined to fashion a goal that was made on the Hammers' training ground and the understanding they had forged there.

Ray Wilson found Peters down the left, and he whipped in a curling cross that seemed to hang in the air before Hurst met it at the near post with a perfectly timed run and superbly weighted glancing header that beat Argentina goalkeeper Antonio Roma and flew into the net. 'The best England goal I ever saw in my time with the squad,' was Bobby Charlton's verdict. 'An unstoppable cross and header.'

England were into the semi-finals, and Hurst would play a big part in helping them negotiate that hurdle too. He missed three early openings before Bobby Charlton put England ahead against Portugal but played a key role in extending their advantage, with his intelligence instrumental in Charlton's crucial second goal.

Watch it back now and it seems deceptively simple but it is actually made by many of the best parts of Hurst's game combined. When George Cohen knocks a hopeful ball up the pitch into the right-hand channel, Hurst is second-favourite to reach it, but his speed means he gets there just ahead of his marker, just inside the area, and his strength means he is able to turn towards goal and look up, all while thinking about what to do next.

'I spent the first five years of my career at West Ham, doing the donkey work if you like, as a player who wanted to run forward to create space for the team,' remembered Hurst. 'So it was quite a customary thing for me to do.

'The defender who was marking me slightly misread it, it was a little bit of a skiddy top, it had rained prior to the game and I anticipated the ball would skid just past him.

'I managed to nudge my way inside him without fouling him, and gain possession. At that stage I wasn't sure whether to go on and shoot, but I saw Bobby joining me from midfield and I just rolled it very gently into his path. And of course rolling the ball that slow for Bobby to hit, I mean, it was only going to finish up in one place, in the back of the net.'

Despite a late rally by Portugal, England held on to win 2–1. Hurst had not scored, but his performance, and especially that assist, ensured he kept his place despite Greaves being fit for the final.

Team-mates for West Ham and England (from left): Bobby Moore, Martin Peters and Geoff Hurst.

A 1960s bubble gum trading card of Geoff Hurst, or Geof as he is called here – even World Cup winners can get their names misspelt.

'I will always believe the ball was over the line.' *– Geoff Hurst*

His selection remains a talking point decades on but so, of course, does the way he justified Ramsey's faith in him. By now, Hurst was confident that he belonged in the England team, but even in his wildest dreams he could not have anticipated what would happen next, starting with a timely equaliser.

West Germany's early opener had been a big blow, even though the team who scored first had not won any of the four post-war World Cup finals, but Hurst ensured England were not behind for long. His alertness meant he was ready for Moore's quickly taken free-kick and his clever run left him completely unmarked to head past Hans Tilkowski and make it 1–1.

With 12 minutes to go, England thought they had scored the winner and again Hurst was involved. His shot from Alan Ball's corner hit Wolfgang Weber and fell for Peters, who made no mistake from six yards.

Without the intervention of Swiss referee Gottfried Dienst, that would have wrapped up the World Cup and perhaps the inventive Peters, whom Ramsey later described as being a player who was '10 years ahead of his time' because of his ability to appear late in the box to score, would be the one celebrated in this book.

Instead, with a minute to go, Dienst decided Jack Charlton had fouled Uwe Seeler when he climbed above him to win a header. West Germany scored the scrappiest of goals from the resulting free-kick to take the game to extra-time, and it was Hurst who ended up earning worldwide fame.

His second goal of the game, to put England 3–2 up in the 11th minute of extra-time, is memorable enough, mainly because it is disputed to this day. Alan Ball was the creator, haring past a tiring Karl-Heinz Schnellinger and finding Hurst, who takes a touch before swivelling to hammer his shot against the underside of the bar and, depending on who you believe, either on to or just over the goal line.

The referee Dienst was unsure whether the whole ball had crossed the line but, famously, the Russian lineman Tofiq Bahramov, who was actually from Azerbaijan, was convinced it had. So was Hurst.

'I will always believe the ball was over the line,' Hurst told the BBC in 1999. 'To back that

England were back in front, but Hurst's incredible day was not done.

up, the person with the best view was Roger Hunt, who was following up, and I maintain this – instinctively in sport, if you are not sure the ball is over the line, you attempt to put it back in.

'Instead, Roger shouted "it's a goal, it's there," he put his right arm in the air and wheeled away and that has always been good enough for me.'

England were back in front, but Hurst's incredible day was not done. With only seconds left, Moore picked him out and he found himself bearing down on goal, with the chance to make absolutely certain of victory.

To his right, Ball has made up ground and is yelling for a pass inside, which stops a defender coming across to challenge Hurst. He appears to be exhausted but makes it to just inside the area before letting fly with a rocket shot into the roof of the net, with the last kick of the match.

'The thing about the force of the shot is if you look at the film of it, the stills of it, just on that spot where I shot, it had started to cut up and actually the ball bobbled up fractionally, almost set up like a tee at golf,' Hurst later explained. 'I didn't catch it on the end of my foot towards the toes, I caught it right on the bony hard instep, and that's why it sort of flew in the net.'

While the country celebrated, Hurst went home. When the world's media arrived at his house the day after the final, they found him mowing the lawn and cleaning his car.

'You went back to normal life very quickly,' Hurst recalled in 2011. 'There was only about a week between the end of the World Cup and the start of the next season. You didn't have a great deal of a chance to celebrate and enjoy that because A) you didn't realise how big it was in a sense, and B) within a week we were back training and playing.'

'Normal' for Hurst meant continuing to score goals for West Ham, and he also kept his England place, leading the line for Ramsey's England for the next six years. His highlights included another hat-trick in a thumping 5–0 win over France in 1969, a trademark thunderbolt penalty against Scotland later that year and the only goal of England's

Hurst's header for England's equaliser in the World Cup final (top) is never doubted but to this day people constantly question whether his shot to make it 3–2 actually crossed the line after smashing the underside of the crossbar and flying downwards. The reaction of his team-mate Roger Hunt, who is shown here (bottom) wheeling away in celebration rather than looking to fire the rebound home, is often used as evidence the ball was in.

Hurst is reunited with the World Cup final hat-trick ball and the crossbar that helped him score his second goal that day. Both items are on display at the National Football Museum in Manchester.

opening game of the 1970 World Cup finals, against Romania.

He scored his last international goal in a 2–0 win over Greece in Athens in December 1971, a week before his 30th birthday. This saw England qualify for the knockout stages of the European Championship, but an unhappy night at Wembley saw them lose the first leg of their quarter-final to West Germany the following spring.

Hurst was replaced by Rodney Marsh with 20 minutes to go during a 3–1 defeat, and that proved to be his final appearance for his country. He was named in the squad for the return in Berlin but was forced to pull out because of injury.

Further honours eluded him at club level too. Although he reached the League Cup semi-finals with West Ham in 1972, he had a penalty saved by Stoke

City goalkeeper Gordon Banks late in the second leg, which Hurst would later describe as the biggest regret of his career.

The Potters eventually prevailed after two replays, going on to win the competition. Hurst joined them later that year, helping them to two successive fifth-place finishes in the old Division One, a feat they have only bettered once before or since.

It might have been a different story for Hurst had Manchester United succeeded in their attempt to sign him in 1967, after he had followed up his World Cup heroics by scoring 29 goals in 41 league games and a total of 35 in 49 matches in all competitions.

Matt Busby, United's manager, phoned from Poland, where they were playing in the European Cup, with an offer of £200,000 to sign him for the reigning league champions, which would have been a British record fee, but Greenwood, who was still in charge at West Ham, replied with a famous telegram, that simply read 'Busby, Manchester United, Gornik, No. Greenwood'.

Greenwood was such an admirer that when he was appointed England boss in 1977, he asked Hurst, who after spells with West

> He scored his last international goal in a 2–0 win over Greece in Athens in December 1971 . . .

Brom, Cork Celtic in Ireland and Seattle Sounders in the United States was player-manager of Telford United in the Southern League, to take coaching sessions to demonstrate what he wanted to see from England's strikers.

He was also part of Greenwood's coaching staff at the 1980 European Championship and 1982 World Cup, and had a two-year stint as Chelsea manager between 1979 and 1981. He left after failing to steer the club into the top flight, and other than a spell coaching Kuwait between 1982 and 1984, that was the end of his career in the dugout.

Hurst had more success after moving into the insurance business, and also endorsed double-glazing and worked as an after-dinner speaker. He was knighted in 1998 and worked as an ambassador for England's unsuccessful bid to host the 2006 World Cup, while waiting with the rest of us for a Three Lions team to win one again.

No Englishman has scored more goals at World Cups than Gary Lineker, who found the net a total of 10 times at the 1986 and 1990 finals.

Gary Lineker

Born	30 November 1960
Place of birth	Leicester
Position	Centre-forward

Gary Lineker scored 48 goals in 80 games for England between 1984 and 1992, including a record 10 goals at World Cup finals. He was the leading scorer in the English top flight on three different occasions, each time with a different club – Leicester, Everton and Tottenham. Former England manager Bobby Robson described him as 'simply the best finisher I have ever seen' and his sportsmanship was also exemplary – he was never booked in his entire senior career of over 600 club or international games.

England's greatest goalscorer of his generation based on the number of times he found the net was also the finest finisher in terms of the ease he did so.

Gary Lineker was the archetypal penalty area poacher, or fox in the box, with a reputation for effortless finishing and an easy-going nature, but his placid demeanour belied the ambition, intelligence and hard work that made him world class. It was no coincidence he was always able to forensically dissect his craft, because it was the same attention to detail that made him the scourge of so many opposition defences.

A self-confessed late developer who was 25 by the time he established himself at international level, Lineker became England's go-to man when they needed a goal for the big occasion, whether it was at World Cups or in qualifying for major tournaments.

His reputation for repeated rescue acts is one of the reasons his exit from the England scene,

Lineker is all smiles after his hat-trick against Poland at the 1986 World Cup.

when he was hauled off during a must-win group game against hosts Sweden at the 1992 European Championship, was so controversial.

It was also in stark contrast to the moment that made him as a marksman, at the Mexico 1986 World Cup, when his stunning 36-minute hat-trick against Poland kept England in the competition.

Their campaign would ultimately end at the hands – well, one hand anyway – of Diego Maradona and Argentina in the quarter-finals but it was in full-blown crisis after a goalless first two games left them bottom of their group and on the brink of an embarrassingly early exit.

A 1–0 defeat by Portugal had been followed by a 0–0 draw with Morocco, memorable only for a serious shoulder injury to skipper Bryan Robson and a red card for Ray Wilkins, who had petulantly thrown the ball at the referee.

That meant nothing less than victory would do against Poland at the Estadio Universitario in Monterrey. Bobby Robson stuck with Lineker, who was by now on a run of six matches without a goal, but chose to pair him with the guile of Peter Beardsley rather than the physical presence of Mark Hateley. It took just over seven minutes for their partnership to spark and change the mood from desperation to delight.

To watch the game back now is to witness an exquisite example of the art of a striker, starting with the first goal. Lineker and Beardsley combine on a swift break forward before feeding the ball to Trevor Steven, who finds a galloping Gary Stevens making up ground down the right. When he fires in a low cross, Lineker, loping in from the left, times his sprint to the near post to perfection.

'He got in front of his man!' exclaims a joyful BBC commentator Barry Davies as Lineker appears in the right place to expertly sweep the ball home and, six minutes later, he has another goal to gleefully describe. This time it is Steve Hodge who provides a bouncing ball into the box from the left and Lineker does not have to break his stride to bury it into the back of the net. 'Magnificent!' is Davies' verdict.

The goal that wraps up the win and completes Lineker's hat-trick, all before half-time, is more of a gift, after Polish goalkeeper Józef Mlynarczyk inexplicably drops a corner practically at Lineker's feet, but it is still gratefully received, with another instinctive finish into the roof of the net.

'He says thank you very much,' was how Davies saw it from the striker's perspective. England's World Cup was up and running, and life for Lineker was never quite the same again.

'I think that was the most important match in my whole career because it just turned things round,' he told the BBC in 1999. 'If I hadn't scored in that game, and we had been knocked out, I probably would never have played for England again.

'That would have been my seventh game without a goal and people would have said "well, he can't do it." It is such a fine line between success and failure.'

That game made Lineker a worldwide star, something he admitted appeared unlikely at the start of his career, even if he was always a prolific scorer who hit 161 goals in one season for his primary school Under-11 team.

The son of a fruit and vegetable merchant – his dad ran the family business, which was founded by Gary's great grandfather, at Leicester open-air market – Lineker was obsessed by football as a boy but was unsure if he was truly good enough to make the grade.

'I really wanted to be,' he reflected later. 'Fortunately I had the natural ability, call it what you may, to help me along my way.'

A season ticket holder with his local side, Leicester City, he found out the Foxes wanted to sign him, aged 13, when he got home from playing for his Sunday team, Aylestone Park Under-14s.

His grandfather broke the news, telling him that during the game he had started talking to the club's chief scout, Ray Shaw, who told him he was watching the centre-forward . . . Lineker.

From there he signed schoolboy forms, trained twice a week after school for two years and was then taken on as an apprentice, despite interest from Chelsea and Celtic, who had also approached his parents. Lineker had also played cricket for Leicester and Midlands Schools until Under-15 level, but football received his full focus from then on.

His main attribute at this stage was raw speed – he was Leicestershire Schools 400 m champion – but his strength was somewhat lacking. Although a surprising number of his goals for club and country would come with his head, he was never the tallest or most powerful of strikers – at his peak he weighed 12st 5lb and stood 5ft 9in – but, when he left school aged 16, Lineker was just 5ft 6in tall and weighed less than nine stone.

While he was fleet-footed, he was frequently knocked off the ball too easily so the club put him on an intense weight-training course, fed him steaks and told him to drink bottle after bottle of milk. It worked, but it took time for him to fill out.

Lineker was still lightweight when he signed his first full-time contract two years later but aged 18 he could run 100 m in 10.5 seconds and that lightning pace helped him break into the Foxes' first team, albeit out wide rather than up front.

After making his senior debut in the old Division Two against Oldham on New Year's Day 1979 – 'I remember it very clearly because it was a frosty pitch and I was awful. It was four months before I played again' – he would go on to play his first 30 games for Leicester as a right winger.

Once he was switched back to centre-forward, the goals began to flow. His secret was a tremendous acceleration, allied by a willingness to gamble by guessing where the ball might break for him in the box and a work ethic that meant he kept making those moves time and again.

Lineker always preferred to play down any talk of him having

Lineker joined J-League side Grampus Eight in 1992 at the launch of football as a professional sport in Japan.

a sixth sense that allowed him to find space in the six-yard box for his trademark close-range finishes, instead referring to the countless fruitless runs he made when the pass he anticipated never came.

'Goalscoring is like mathematics,' he said in 2023. 'It's a formula, it's not instinct. Most players wait to see where the ball is going to go, and then it's too late, but it's about making runs constantly into the space where you think you might score a goal if the ball goes there. It's the law of probability that means you eventually get a great chance to score a goal.'

The goals certainly added up for Lineker, who scored 22 in Division One for Leicester in 1983–84. They brought him his first England call-up, for a British Home Championship game against Wales at the end of that campaign. He did not play, but manager Bobby Robson had heard good things about him and wanted to see the striker for himself.

'I spoke to Gerry Summers, the Leicester coach, about Gary and he told me one or two things about him that pleased me,' Robson recalled. 'He said he was going to be a prospect for the future, that he was going to be a goalscorer and maybe prolific. He was quick over five yards, he could read defenders, he could get behind defenders, he was very alive and quick to the ball in the box.'

Lineker impressed Robson in training and kept his place in his squad that faced Scotland a few weeks later. This time, he did get on the pitch, making his senior debut as a substitute for Tony Woodcock when he came on for the final 17 minutes of a 1–1 draw at Hampden Park, but although he kept scoring for Leicester the following season, he had to wait a while for his next England chance.

Woodcock, Trevor Francis, Mark Hateley, Paul Mariner, Clive Allen, Peter Withe and Luther Blissett were all picked ahead of him to lead the line before, nine games and 10 months later, Lineker got his next cap and first start, against the Republic of Ireland in March 1985. He marked it with a goal of genuine class, latching on to a perfectly weighted Peter Davenport pass on the edge of the area and composing himself to clip the ball over Packie Bonner to score the second goal in a 2–1 win.

'I've watched the goal a few times. It was a pivotal, seminal moment of my career,' Lineker said in 2015. 'It was a great ball from Peter and quite a cool finish, one I liked quite a lot. It was an amazing feeling to not only score for England but getting my first goal, and at Wembley, was something I will never forget.'

More landmark moments followed, including his first Golden Boot after finishing as joint-leading scorer in Division One with Chelsea's Kerry Dixon on 24 goals, and the pair of them kept on scoring when they were partnered up front for England against West Germany and the United States on their summer tour.

'Goalscoring is like mathematics. It's a formula, it's not instinct.' – *Gary Lineker*

By now, Lineker was an Everton player after the league champions pounced to sign him for £800,000. His first task at Goodison Park was to win over the

Lineker puts Everton ahead in the 1986 FA Cup final, but Liverpool fought back to win 3–1.

How it ended. Lineker is substituted in his final England appearance, a 2–1 defeat by Sweden at the 1992 European Championship.

fans who adored his predecessor, the charismatic Scottish target-man Andy Gray, a more complete striker when you consider his contribution outside the box, but a much less prolific one.

Lineker's determination and sheer weight of goals helped him settle in on Merseyside, and almost took the team to even greater heights. He ended with a tally of 30 goals in 41 league games, scored five more in the FA Cup and another three in the League Cup, but despite being eight points above eventual champions Liverpool in February, Everton would end the season empty-handed.

A late surge by the Reds took them to the title and they also beat their neighbours in the FA Cup final to seal the Double at Wembley, when Lineker had put Everton ahead before half-time but Liverpool hit back with three second-half goals. The only accolades he ended up with were individual ones: as well as ending up top scorer in England for a second successive year, he was also voted Footballer of the Year.

That was enough to attract the attention of Barcelona – the story that they came calling after his heroics in Mexico is a myth because talks had already started when the World Cup got under way, but those goals against Poland pushed his price up and the £2.2 m fee he eventually commanded made him the second-most expensive player on the planet after Maradona.

'It's not really true to say it was that game that made the transfer, because it was already on,' said Lineker's long-term agent Jon Holmes. 'The only thing Barcelona vice president Joan Gaspart said afterwards was "oh, it'll cost us more money now!"'

As well as increasing his value, Lineker was enhancing his reputation. He scored two more against Paraguay in the last 16 and headed home England's late consolation against Argentina, with only an incredible goal-line clearance from Julio Olarticoechea denying him an equaliser in an infamous last-eight defeat.

Still, the six goals that gave him the Golden Boot in Mexico meant Lineker was a global superstar by the time he arrived in Spain, so it is worth remembering that he almost missed the tournament full stop.

He had fallen heavily on his left wrist in England's final warm-up game against Canada but a hospital examination showed he had suffered a severe sprain rather than a fracture. He was able to play, with his wrist heavily strapped – something that is only noticeable now because that arm is held aloft for each of his celebrations.

Despite all this success, Lineker still did not have the supreme self-confidence you might associate with such a ruthless striker. In fact, he says he did not lose the self-doubt he'd had since he was a child until several months later. At the start of 1987, he started his first El Clasico against Real Madrid and scored a hat-trick in front of 120,000 fans at Camp Nou, then, less than three weeks later, hit four goals for England against Spain at the Bernabéu.

'I used to think every level I got to, they'd find me out,' he said later. 'That is when it dawned on me that I was good at this.

'At this point I was probably the best goalscorer in the world. I wasn't a great footballer but I could certainly stick the ball away.'

There were clouds on the horizon, however, initially for England. Illness denied him the chance to play at the peak of his powers at the 1988 European

Championship, where Robson's side lost all three of their group games. Lineker's personal poor performances were explained afterwards when he was diagnosed with hepatitis – he was hospitalised for a week and took months to make a full recovery.

That affected his fortunes at club level too. He had a new manager at Barca, Johan Cruyff, and when Lineker finally returned to fitness he found himself playing where he had started his professional career, out on the right wing, and it became obvious he would soon be on the move again.

Bayern Munich, Genoa, Fiorentina, PSV Eindhoven and a host of English clubs, including Everton and Queens Park Rangers, all showed interest in 1989 but an expected bid from Italian giants Juventus never came.

Instead it was left to Holmes to instigate a reunion with the man who had signed Lineker for Barcelona, Terry Venables, who was now in charge of Tottenham. Despite a late bid from Manchester United, Lineker was on his way to north London for £1.1 m, and marked his return to England by becoming the First Division's leading scorer for a third time, with 24 goals.

His next World Cup, in Italy in 1990, was also a success as England reached the last four, although not before surviving a scare against Cameroon, who led 2–1 with seven minutes of a helter-skelter quarter-final clash to go.

Lineker proved the saviour again, calmly putting away a penalty to equalise after being brought down in the box, then repeating the trick in extra-time to send England through. The two spot-kicks were very different – the first was slotted to the keeper's left, the second slammed down the middle – but crucially they both ended up in the net.

'You don't feel that cool,' he told the BBC in 2024 when asked whether he was feeling the pressure. 'It's a bit like a duck on the water – they appear calm on the surface but they are flapping underneath. I'd been on penalties for England for five years without actually getting to take one but I was pretty confident because I took 40 to 50 a day in training.'

He scored another vital late equaliser against West Germany in the semi-final, this time from open play, for his fourth goal of the tournament, and was also successful in the shootout but to no avail. Stuart Pearce saw his effort saved, Chris Waddle missed, and England were out.

Although Lineker had lifted the Copa del Rey with Barcelona in 1988 and followed that up by clinching the now defunct European Cup Winners' Cup in 1989, he had won surprisingly little by this stage and that would be the closest he got to a major trophy with England.

He did get his hands on some silverware with Spurs the following season, however, helping them overcome Nottingham Forest in a classic FA Cup final, albeit one tainted by seeing his talented team-mate Paul Gascoigne

The expert finisher – Lineker scores the goal against Poland that booked England's place at Euro '92.

Lineker won the Copa del Rey and the European Cup Winners' Cup with Barcelona, but his only success in England was winning the 1991 FA Cup with Tottenham.

> 'I never won a league title, so to win the FA Cup was very special.'
> – *Gary Lineker*

hospitalised after a disastrous early challenge on Gary Charles.

'I never won a league title, so to win the FA Cup was very special,' Lineker said. 'I'd put Everton in front in the 1986 final but we ended up losing, so it was a relief to finally get my hands on the trophy.

'While I didn't score, I had a perfectly good goal disallowed and missed a penalty. It didn't matter because we won 2–1. We celebrated by visiting Gazza in hospital after he injured himself with that rash tackle.'

More goals would follow for Tottenham, but that was Lineker's final taste of glory as a player and sadly his international career would have an especially unhappy ending.

Graham Taylor had taken over from Bobby Robson in 1990 and made Lineker his captain but their relationship soon deteriorated even though he continued to find the net for his country, including a spectacular late strike against Poland in November 1991 that maintained his reputation as the nation's golden boy, and ensured England qualified for the 1992 European Championship.

He scored one more England goal, against the CIS – a team made up of the Commonwealth of Independent States that replaced the Soviet Union – but missed the chance to equal Bobby Charlton's all-time scoring record of 49 goals for England when his ill-judged and weak Panenka penalty against Brazil at Wembley in May 1992 was easily saved by Carlos Roberto.

'It was a friendly, it was against Brazil, for the England record. Why didn't I just hit it into the corner?' he would later ask himself.

Taylor was the one being questioned exactly a month later following England's 2–1 defeat by Sweden that eliminated them from Euro '92. He had hauled Lineker off with 27 minutes remaining and the score at 1–1, a decision that still makes little sense more than three decades on.

Lineker finished his playing days in Japan with Nagoya Grampus Eight, where he was hampered by a persistent toe injury, and moved into broadcasting when he retired in 1994. He presented *Match of The Day* from 1999 until 2025.

Harry Kane scored 280 goals in 435 games for Tottenham before joining Bayern Munich in 2023.

11

HARRY KANE

Born	28 July 1993
Place of birth	Walthamstow, London
Position	Centre-forward

Harry Kane has been England's record men's goalscorer since surpassing Wayne Rooney's total of 53 goals in 2023, the same year he ended a 19-year stay with Tottenham by joining Bayern Munich. Kane, who is also Spurs' all-time leading scorer, won the Golden Boot at the 2018 World Cup and shared the same award at the 2024 European Championship. He has topped the Premier League scoring charts three times.

There is a photograph of an 11-year-old Harry Kane standing alongside his idol David Beckham at the launch of Beckham's Football Academy at London's Buoy Wharf in 2005 that might suggest the story of how he went on to become a superstar striker was a smooth one; another player who was spotted early, always stood out and seemed destined to sail straight to the very summit of his sport.

The actual tale of Kane's journey from when he was first scouted to becoming a talismanic figure for club and country is anything but straightforward, however, even if he had inspiration on his doorstep – he grew up in the same part of east London, Chingford, as Beckham had done a couple of decades earlier.

'Seeing David go on to achieve what he did made it seem a little more real,' Kane told the Football Association in 2023. 'If I didn't have that, I might have felt it was out of reach or an impossible task with so many people and potential footballers out there, but it gave me that little bit of extra belief that I could go on and achieve the same.'

The similarities only go so far, however. While they both practised for hours with their parents in the same parks, went to the same secondary school and even played for the same junior team, Ridgeway Rovers, Kane's eventual path to the top would be completely different from the one his hero took.

Just like Beckham, Kane did have something special but, rather than skill or technique, being physically strong or especially quick, it was his self-belief in front of goal and in his ability overall that helped him make the grade – although, as a late bloomer, his progress still did not follow any script.

'I first saw him when he was six. The thing with Harry is he just had so much confidence even then,' Kane's first coach with Ridgeway Rovers, Dave Bricknell, told *The Independent* newspaper in 2021. 'He never dwelled on misses. If he missed, he knew there was another chance coming soon.'

That mindset of always looking ahead to his next opportunity was what helped Kane cope when he tasted rejection as a junior, and his strong mentality also helped him keep his focus through a testing sequence of loan moves in his early years as a professional, an unforgiving environment that not every budding player survives.

His progress through the Premier League's academy system, receiving hours of expert coaching at purpose-built facilities first at Arsenal and then at Tottenham, was more structured than the schooling Beckham got as a young boy, and was a world away from the experience of most England players from the eras that preceded his, who learnt the game on the streets or with their friends in the park.

Still, what he had in common with those ghostly stars of England's past, from Eddie Hapgood to Gordon Banks, was an obsession with self-improvement, along with the dedication, drive and determination to overcome any knockbacks, such as the one he was given when he was released by Arsenal aged nine, after two years struggling to survive, let alone shine, in their academy.

Kane returned to grassroots football and Sunday league with his schoolfriends for 18 months before signing for Tottenham aged 11 although, given he was short and stocky compared to his peers, they did not feel they had

Kane celebrates his first goal for England, seconds after he came off the bench to make his debut against Lithuania in 2015.

‘That boy at 13, who didn’t have everything, taught himself an awful lot more . . .’
– Alex Inglethorpe

a world-beater in the making. Initially they rejected him too, before changing their minds when he scored a hat-trick against them while on trial for Watford.

‘One of the coaches said to me bluntly “who is that fat kid?”,’

Kane scores for Bayern Munich in their Champions League last-16 tie against Lazio in March 2024.

recalled Richard Allen, former head of academy recruitment at Spurs, when asked about Kane's first days at the club. 'Harry was 11 at the time, and the truth is he would not have got in the building if we were using physical testing as a determinant.'

Alex Inglethorpe, a lower league journeyman striker turned youth development guru who became director of Tottenham's academy before taking the same role at Liverpool, coached Spurs' under-14 team when Kane was 13, and says it was his mentality that stood out.

'I'd like to say that he was the gold medallist in the group and that we'd always spotted he was going to be the fantastic player, but that's not the case, I'd be lying,' Inglethorpe told the BBC in 2016. 'He probably wasn't even on the podium.

'He had a lot of growing still to come, but he had lovely technique at that age, so that was probably the thing you hooked into first and foremost when you saw him – he definitely had an ability to pass and receive and to shoot – but if there was something that endeared you to him when he worked, it was that he was very, very low maintenance.

'He was a football obsessive even then and someone who was quietly unassuming and had a desire to improve. He had the attributes more around character and technique but he wasn't one of the group who you would think was a natural England player or Premier League player at that time.'

Kane was a hard worker, and versatile too. He had volunteered to go in goal on his first trial for Ridgeway Rovers and he was still playing in multiple positions when he signed a scholarship contract with Spurs on his 16th birthday in July 2009, lining up for their youth teams in midfield and on the right wing as well as up front, which was the role he would make his own.

'It became fairly evident when Harry became a scholar that he was someone who could finish,' Inglethorpe added. He wasn't great then with his head or on his left side, but he has been his own best coach.

'That boy at 13, who didn't have everything, taught himself an awful lot more in those five years that followed. He was very aware of what he didn't have, and very aware of what might stop him – and he was very determined to make that right.'

The lessons got even harder as Spurs shipped Kane out on a series of loan moves to lower league clubs between 2011 and 2013.

Not all of them worked out, but as well as developing physically, the important thing was that he was still willing to learn.

At this stage, Kane was not only honing the craft of a goal-hungry striker, he was perfecting the art of being a complete forward, and evolving the parts of his game that would become his trademark: how to come short, hold up the ball and link play by bringing others into the game, as well as retaining a selfish streak and shooting on sight from any angle in front of goal.

He made his professional debut at 17, coming on for League One side Leyton Orient as a 73rd-minute substitute in a 1–1 draw at Rochdale on 15 January 2011, but only found his scoring form when he joined Millwall for another short spell a year later. His next stop, Norwich, supposedly for a season, was ruined by injury, then he spent most of his stint at Leicester on the bench.

'It was all part of his development,' remembers QPR's technical director Chris Ramsey, one of his former coaches who was Tottenham's head of player development during that period. 'Not every loan you go on works out, but it helped him be more resilient and work out what he needed to do when he played. We never really looked at those loans as failures, more as a learning curve.'

Kane was still getting some sniffs of first-team action with Spurs at this stage, and scored his first goal for the club against Shamrock Rovers in the Europa League in 2011, but his breakthrough moment with Tottenham did not arrive until Tim Sherwood, who had been in charge of the academy when Kane was coming through the ranks, took over from André Villas-Boas as manager for the final few months of the 2013–14 season.

Sherwood, who felt Kane's dual qualities as goal maker and scorer made him 'a mix between Teddy Sheringham and Alan Shearer', handed him his first Premier League start, against Sunderland in April 2014. Kane, who was three months away from his 21st birthday, scored in a 5–1 win.

'I had made a few late cameos before that game, but I saw my first start as a chance to prove that I could do it at that level,' Kane told *FourFourTwo* in 2024.

'To score and win the game set me off on a good run of scoring – from there, things just went up

Kane scores his second goal of the game to give England a 2–1 win over Tunisia in their opening game of the 2018 World Cup.

'I saw my first start as a chance to prove that I could do it at that level.' – *Harry Kane*

and up. I always look back at that game and wonder what might have happened if I hadn't played so well and if I hadn't scored.'

There were even more obstacles to overcome, however. Kane had to prove himself all over again to his next manager Mauricio Pochettino, who replaced Sherwood that summer. Despite him starting the following season by scoring in both legs of a Europa League qualifying tie with Cypriot side AEL Limassol, Pochettino was initially unconvinced.

'On September 18 (2014), Harry played at Partizan Belgrade, but he struggled and we drew 0–0,' Pochettino told the BBC during the 2022 World Cup. 'Three days later, when we played West Brom, I didn't even put him on the bench. That week, Harry came to see me and my coaching staff. He thought he deserved to play more.

'We showed Harry, with video clips and with stats, that he was wrong. We had to show Harry he still needed to improve in different areas, how he still needed to wait and to prove to us

Kane secured England's qualification for the 2018 World Cup with his goal in their 1–0 win over Slovenia at Wembley in October 2017.

that he was better than his teammates and he deserved to start.

'It was a really tough conversation, but it was also a really good conversation. Players never want to be told the truth. It's never easy when you have to tell a player that they are wrong, but it was a case of trying to help him by being tough on him.'

It worked. Kane embarked on a run of seven goals in his next seven games that culminated in him coming off the bench to score a last-minute deflected free-kick winner against Aston Villa at the start of November, for his first Premier League goal. Pochettino admitted it kept him in his job, and it was also a huge turning point for Kane, because he became Spurs' first-choice striker for the first time.

'From that point on, Harry got to the level we expected and showed in every single game why we believed in him,' Pochettino recalled. 'Very, very quickly, he became one of the best strikers in the Premier League.'

Kane ended the campaign with 21 league goals, and 31 in all competitions, as he helped Spurs to a fifth-place finish and to reach the League Cup final, where they lost to Chelsea.

He was named the Professional Footballers' Association's Young Player of the Year and ended the campaign in the full England squad. For someone who had made such a slow start to his club career, he did not take long to make his mark at international level once he was given the chance.

England boss Roy Hodgson named him in his squad to play Lithuania in a Euro 2016 qualifier on 27 March 2015 and brought him on for Wayne Rooney with 20 minutes to go . . . just 79 seconds later, and with only his third touch, Kane headed in a Raheem Sterling cross to make it 4–0.

When Kane was asked in 2024 to choose the games that changed his life, this was one of his picks. 'Playing for England means the world to me, so I have to choose my debut,' he explained. 'It was a magical moment to do it at Wembley – to score at that stadium, in front of my friends and family, was just everything I had dreamed of as a boy growing up.

'I remember being told by the manager that I was going to come on for the last 20 minutes and feeling like everything that had happened to me in my whole life had led up to that moment.

'I was a ball of nerves and energy, but also felt ready to take my chance. To mark my debut on the international stage with a goal inside two minutes of coming on was very special. Playing for England still always gives me that buzz, no matter how many times I get picked. You never lose that pride.'

His England career was up and running, and he could not stop scoring at club level either. Numbers alone cannot do justice to a player's influence on a team – there are no statistics that show character or reflect bravery, for example – but, for strikers, goals are a currency of their own and in that sense Kane proved priceless by sustaining his astonishing scoring rate over the following few seasons.

He was the Premier League's leading scorer in 2015–16 and 2016–17 and, although Liverpool's Mohamed Salah pipped him to that prestigious honour the following year, Kane's tally of 30 league goals was his best yet.

'Scoring for England is something that will stay with you forever . . .'
– Harry Kane

Things got even better for him that summer when, as England captain, he scored six goals to help them reach the semi-finals at the 2018 World Cup and became only the third Englishman to win a Golden Boot at a major tournament, following Gary Lineker at the 1986 World Cup and Alan Shearer at the 1996 European Championship.

His success in Russia – starting with two goals, including a 91st-minute winner, in an opening-game win over Tunisia – elevated his profile beyond the Premier League and wiped out the miserable memory of his major tournament debut at the 2016 European Championship, when Kane had failed to score and was controversially asked to take corners.

'Russia was my first World Cup, the biggest competition in the world and the highest pressure you can feel in football,' Kane explained to *FourFourTwo* magazine. 'To go out there in my first game on that stage and score two goals, including the winning goal in the last minute, put me on a bigger platform and made people around the world take notice.

'We went on to have a decent tournament, reaching the semi-finals, and that moment of scoring

Kane is in the right place again to put England ahead against Denmark at Euro 2024.

a last-minute goal in a World Cup – a tournament that I have been watching my whole life – was just incredible. Scoring for England is something that will stay with you forever, especially the ones in the big tournaments, and the big matches.'

Kane did more of the same at Euro 2020, although he had to wait until the knockout stages to open his account. For the first time in his international career, his selection was being questioned, but he responded with four goals in three games.

He started with a goal against Germany in the last 16, hit two more in a quarter-final win over Ukraine and then scored an extra-time winner against Denmark in the semi-final, putting away the rebound after his penalty was saved.

That fired England into their first major final for 55 years, but Kane could not prevent the pain of defeat to Italy on penalties and there was more heartbreak for him at the 2022 World Cup, where he missed a late spot-kick

> 'It's a magical moment and I am really proud.'
> *– Harry Kane*

as England lost a tense quarter-final to France in Qatar.

Major trophies eluded him with Tottenham too, where he lost the Champions League final to Liverpool in 2019 and was also beaten in the League Cup final in 2015 and 2021, but there was soon some consolation in the shape

Kane the record-breaker – his penalty against Italy in March 2023 took him clear of Wayne Rooney as England's record goalscorer.

of major goalscoring landmarks for club and then country.

In February 2023, Kane crashed a first-time finish past Manchester City goalkeeper Ederson to beat the great Jimmy Greaves's tally of 266 goals for Spurs and a few weeks later he wrote himself into the history books with England too.

When he stepped up to calmly put away a penalty in a World Cup qualifying win over Italy, he passed Wayne Rooney's total of 53 goals and became England's all-time top scorer. The feat had taken him only 81 games – 39 fewer than Rooney.

'It means everything,' Kane said afterwards. 'It had to be a penalty, I had a feeling it would be, but I've prepared well for it and thankfully I put it away. Once it hit the back of the net, there was huge emotion. It's a magical moment and I am really proud.'

Within a matter of months, he was on the move. Kane had been linked with a big-money move away from Tottenham for many years, to Real Madrid or Manchester City, but by the time he did finally leave, in an £86 m move to Bayern Munich in August 2023, he had plundered a total of 280 goals in 435 appearances for the club, including 213 on the Premier League stage. Only Shearer, with 260, has more.

Which were his favourites? 'It's hard to say,' he told *The Guardian* newspaper. 'A couple against Arsenal at the old White Hart Lane – in my first north London derby, the header, and then the one where I bent it in from the left, [off the] post and in. Those two stick in my memory.'

Kane settled quickly in Germany, scoring 44 goals in 45 games in his first season with Bayern, but he could not maintain that form at the 2024 European Championship, where England again went agonisingly close to ending their long wait for glory.

He started every game and scored three goals that gave him a share of the Golden Boot, but more criticism came his way for his performances, as he appeared short of full fitness and was unable to make any impact against Spain in the final.

His goals and individual accolades mean his legacy with England is already secure, but his search for a crowning moment with his country goes on.

Honourable Mentions

Choosing only 11 players as Immortals of English football was no easy task, and this elite group of greats could easily have been expanded if the numbers had not been severely limited for the purposes of selecting a team.

Every supremely talented side has an accomplished bench, however, especially in the modern era when football is so often said to be a squad game, so here are 11 substitutes who deserve recognition as honourable mentions at the very least.

No doubt many of them would be included in the starting XI of other people's lists and it is actually striking to see their similarities – in their ability, application or achievements – to the people preferred ahead of them.

If this book was being written in 10 years' time, I suspect there would be many more present-day players who have earned Immortal status, or at the very least hold a strong claim to it, given how feats at international finals were used as key criteria for inclusion and how close England have come to winning one with their current crop.

From the team who helped the Three Lions reach the final of the 2024 European Championship, Jude Bellingham and Bukayo Saka leap out as young stars who have already shone brightly on the biggest stage, while Phil Foden will surely have a campaign at a major tournament for England that defines him in the same way his performances, goals, assists and trophy-haul have already done for Manchester City.

Their time will come, but for now there are plenty more players to pick from the past for this, surely the best bench in England's history.

As we did with the main selection, let's begin with the last line of defence. More than 100 men have played in goal for England since 1872, many with distinction, but there is only one outstanding candidate to be considered as a back-up to Gordon Banks.

Peter Shilton featured at five major tournaments for England.

Peter Shilton ended up replacing Banks in the national team, just as he had done at club level with Leicester City, and after making his England debut in 1970 went on to win a staggering 125 caps over the next 20 years, a men's record that still stands.

He might have won many more but for a decision by England manager Ron Greenwood to alternate him as first-choice with his great rival Ray Clemence between 1977 and 1982, at a time when Shilton was securing the biggest prizes possible in club football. He won the League title with newly-promoted Nottingham Forest in 1977–78 and followed that by collecting the European Cup in the next two seasons.

Shilton was still regarded as being among the world's best during the next decade, playing at each World Cup between 1982 and 1990, and the poise and presence behind the consistent performances that marked his later years surely owed something to the advice about balance and foot movement he took from a ballroom dancer early in his career.

In contrast, our next player was known for his grit and determination rather than any grace on the pitch. England fans love a warrior and the enduring image everyone has of **Terry Butcher** as Three Lions captain is of him bandaged with his white shirt drenched in blood during a World Cup qualifier against Sweden in 1989.

A first-half clash of heads with Johnny Ekström had left Butcher with a deep cut on his forehead and

Terry Butcher's fearless defending for England saw him inducted in the National Football Museum's Hall of Fame. He is also the only Englishman in the Scottish Football Museum's Hall of Fame, as recognition of his achievements with the Rangers.

some hastily applied stitches failed to hold because of the number of times he headed the ball, but he played on, helping his side get the point they needed to reach Italia 90 the following summer.

It was a performance which summed up Butcher's never-say-die attitude on the pitch but he was known throughout the course of his career for his bravery and leadership qualities as a tough-tackling centre-half who was also dominant in the air.

Butcher won 77 England caps, played at three World Cups for his country and enjoyed success at club level with Ipswich Town, winning the UEFA Cup and twice finishing runners-up in the league, before moving to Scotland with Glasgow Rangers, with whom he won three titles in four seasons.

Then come two more defenders from very different eras, linked by the way the England teams they played for were viewed – harshly – as serious under-achievers.

First up is **Billy Wright**, one of several outstanding players to emerge when competitive football returned in 1946 after the Second World War, who became an almost constant presence for England at wing-half then centre-half.

Billy Wright captained England at the 1950, 1954 and 1958 World Cup finals.

Wright was the first footballer in the world to win 100 caps for his country and played in 70 consecutive internationals between October 1951 and May 1959, so it is no surprise that *The Times* newspaper described him as 'a national treasure'.

Nicknamed 'Mr Dynamo' for his non-stop running, he was also known for his amazing leap and praised by opponents for his sportsmanship – despite his conversion into a defender he never received a booking or red card.

Wright was also arguably the first celebrity footballer, endorsed a string of commercial products, and also had a successful showbiz marriage decades before 'Posh and Becks' when he tied the knot with singer Joy Beverley, of the Beverley Sisters, in 1958.

A one-club man, he made 541 appearances for Wolves between 1939 and 1959, leading them to success in the FA Cup in 1949 and then three league titles when the club were the dominant force in English football in the 1950s.

Although Wright played at three World Cups in the 1950s, at a time when England were always seen as among the favourites, he never got further than the quarter-finals.

Fifty years on, the same fate awaited another gifted group of England players, this time known as 'the Golden Generation', a term actually coined as a reason for optimism by the Football Association's chief executive Adam Crozier in 2001, but which would weigh heavily on the squad.

While they were not world-beaters as a unit, they undoubtedly had several world-class individuals who enjoyed hugely successful careers, one of whom was **Ashley Cole.**

Ashley Cole was only the seventh England player to reach a century of caps.

Cole is England's most capped left-back and also their most capped Black player, making 107 England appearances between 2000 and 2013. There was a time when his speed and positional sense seemed to make him almost impossible to beat and, combined with his attacking ability, made him a formidable force down his flank.

He won nothing with England but he was a serial collector of silverware at club level, including three league titles and a record seven FA Cups.

Another master from the modern era is the first midfielder to be mentioned here, who also made more than a century of England appearances, many as captain.

Steven Gerrard is forever compared with Frank Lampard, who was frequently paired with him in England's midfield, but he gets the nod over his old international team-mate here because he was the more complete player.

A Premier League title always eluded Gerrard, who finished runner-up on three occasions, but he inspired Liverpool to several other successes, many of them almost single-handedly.

His most famous triumph came in the 2005 Champions League final, starting the fightback with the first goal as the Reds came back from 3–0 down to beat AC Milan on penalties.

Similarly, **Paul Scholes** perhaps never reproduced his superb club form when he played for his country, although as he was often shoe-horned into the side on the left of midfield to make space for Gerrard and Lampard, he does at least have a valid excuse.

His best position, from which he could demonstrate his full range of passing and dictate games for Manchester United, was central and much deeper, although he also possessed a powerful shot from distance that brought him dozens of goals.

A modest man, but a magnificent footballer, he won 25 trophies with United, including 11 Premier League titles – more than any other English player – three FA Cups and two Champions League triumphs.

Speaking of creative midfielders who were under-appreciated when they wore an England shirt, **Glenn Hoddle** was often seen as a luxury player on these shores, while being worshipped elsewhere on the continent.

England's first playmaker, before the role was properly recognised in this country, he

Apart from a single season with LA Galaxy before he retired, Steven Gerrard spent his entire playing career with Liverpool.

Paul Scholes started out as a striker before evolving into a gifted playmaker.

Like Scholes, Glenn Hoddle was the most creative English footballer of his generation.

was admired by Johan Cruyff, Diego Maradona, Michel Platini and Ruud Gullit and called 'the most skilful player I ever worked with' by Arsène Wenger.

His exceptional technical ability saw him make and score many goals for Tottenham but there were doubts over his stamina and defensive discipline and people still talked about what he couldn't do, as much as what he could.

While you would never say he wasted his talent, Hoddle could and should have achieved so much more, if any international managers had truly trusted him.

Hoddle's England career still spanned nine years, but that is nothing compared to the final midfielder who makes up our bench, **Sir Stanley Matthews**.

The 'Wizard of the Dribble' made his England debut in 1934 and he played 17 internationals before World War II, including the infamous 'Battle of Highbury' mentioned earlier in this book.

His 42nd and last international cap came 23 years later, at the age of 42, in 1957. One of the game's first superstars, he was the first Footballer of the Year, in 1948, became the first European Footballer of the Year a decade later and then in 1965 he became the first active footballer to be knighted.

A cigarette card from 1939 showing Stanley Matthews, whose international career started before the Second World War and ended in 1957.

Matthews, who played professionally in England's top flight until he was 50, won only one domestic trophy in his entire career, the 1953 FA Cup, when he was 38.

He had lost his previous two finals, in 1948 and 1951, and looked set for a third Wembley defeat when his Blackpool side trailed 3–1 to Bolton in the second half, but Matthews turned the game around in the final half-hour, creating three goals to ensure he finally got his hands on the Cup. His team-mate, Stan Mortensen, scored a hat-trick but the game is remembered as 'The Matthews final' because of the mark he made on it.

Jimmy Greaves was a goalscoring phenomenon.

When it comes to goalscoring feats, few can compare with **Jimmy Greaves,** who scored 44 goals in just 57 games for his country but is forever remembered for the match he missed – the 1966 World Cup final.

He had recovered from the injury that had sidelined him for the previous two knockout ties, but manager Sir Alf Ramsey decided to field an unchanged team. There were no substitutes in those days and, initially, Greaves did not even get a winners' medal despite playing in all three group games, because only the 11 who faced West Germany were eligible. He finally got one in 2009, when FIFA changed their rules.

A natural finisher who still holds the record for the most hat-tricks for his country, six, Greaves also scored at an astonishing rate for Chelsea, AC Milan, Tottenham and West Ham.

He won the FA Cup twice with Spurs, and also helped them collect the European Cup Winners' Cup in 1963, scoring twice as they beat Atletico Madrid.

Greaves finished as top scorer in the old Division One on six occasions between 1959 and 1969, and is the all-time top goalscorer in top flight history with 357, 43 more than the man ranked second on the list, Steve Bloomer.

Alan Shearer is fifth overall with a total of 283, behind Dixie Dean (310) and Gordon Hodgson (288), but leads the way in the Premier League era, which began in 1992, with a record 260 goals that mark him out as the outstanding modern-day striker.

A title-winner with Blackburn Rovers in 1995, his only major team honour, Shearer moved to boyhood club Newcastle United for a world-record fee of £15 m in 1996. As well as being a predatory

Alan Shearer scored 30 goals in 63 appearances for England.

Wayne Rooney retired in 2021 as the all-time leading goalscorer for Manchester United and England, but his record of 53 goals for his country was passed by Harry Kane in 2023.

finisher who was dangerous in the air, he possessed a powerful shot with either foot and many of his goals came from distance.

His best moments with England were at Euro '96, where he scored five goals and was leading scorer, giving him another Golden Boot to go with the three he won for topping the Premier League scoring charts in three consecutive seasons from 1994–95 to 1996–97.

Completing a formidable alternate line-up is **Wayne Rooney**, who was England all-time top scorer between September 2015 and March 2023 and will go down as one of his country's all-time greats.

Rooney was the epitome of a boy-wonder, announcing himself in the Premier League at 16 with a superb goal for Everton against Arsenal in October 2002, and making his senior debut for his country aged 17 years and 111 days in February 2003.

He was still only 18 when he took the 2004 European Championship by storm and many observers felt England would have won that tournament had he not broken his foot early in their quarter-final against Portugal, which ended in defeat on penalties.

Repeating that immense immediate impact in the major finals that followed proved beyond him, with his 2006 World Cup particularly frustrating. He was not fully fit because of another serious foot injury and it would end in acrimony when he was sent off for stamping on Ricardo Carvalho as England again lost a shootout to Portugal in the last eight.

Still, he remained fully committed to his country and ended his international career in 2018 with 53 goals in 120 appearances, the most by any England outfield player.

At club level, he won the Premier League five times after joining Manchester United for £23 m in 2004, at the time a world-record fee for a teenager.

Rooney surpassed Sir Bobby Charlton's scoring record for United in 2017 and is the club's highest all-time scorer with 253 goals, yet his exceptional career still ended with him being accused of not fulfilling his vast potential.

In that sense, it seems appropriate that he is the last to be mentioned here before we sign off – as another example of how the high expectations placed on the most talented English players has seen so many of them judged harshly, even if they up ended up making history.

Beckham takes a corner for Manchester United against Liverpool under the closed roof at the Millennium Stadium, Cardiff, in the 2001 Community Shield. United had won the 2000–01 Premier League title, their third in a row, with Beckham scoring nine league goals and making the most assists of any player: 12.

Bibliography

Sources for cross-referencing statistics for all chapters

BOOKS

Gordon, Jack & Ross, Philip, *England: The Complete Record,* de Coubertin Books, 2018

Matthews, Tony, *England's Who's Who,* Pitch Publishing, 2013

Payne, Mike, *England: The Complete Post-war Record,* Breedon Books, 1993

WEBSITES

EnglandStats.com https://www.englandstats.com/

England Football Online http://www.englandfootballonline.com/

Gordon Banks

BOOKS

Hurst, Geoff, *Geoff Hurst's Greats,* Icon Books, 2016

Banks, Gordon, *Banksy: My Autobiography,* Michael Joseph, 2002

WEBSITES

Pelé on Facebook: https://www.facebook.com/Pele/photos/a.402724329746692/2464155260270245/

Latham-Coyle, Harry, *'Save of the Century' at Euro 2024 hailed by pundits*: https://www.independent.co.uk/sport/football/mert-gunok-save-gordon-banks-turkey-austria-euro-2024-b2573107.html accessed 16 July 2024

Gordon Banks on X: https://x.com/thegordonbanks/status/975602519467528192

Eddie Hapgood

BOOKS

Hapgood, Lynne, *Eddie Hapgood Footballer: From Beyond the Touchline,* Pitch Publishing, 2022

Buchan, Charles, *Charles Buchan: A Lifetime in Football,* Mainstream Publishing, 2010

Hapgood, Eddie, *Football Ambassador: The Autobiography of an Arsenal Legend,* GCR Books, 2009

WEBSITES

Duffy, Jonathan, *Football, Fascism and England's Nazi salute,* http://news.bbc.co.uk/1/hi/magazine/3128202.stm, accessed 5 January 2024

Bobby Moore

BOOKS

Hurst, Geoff, *Geoff Hurst's Greats,* Icon Books, 2014

Giller, Norman, *The World's Greatest Football Matches,* Octopus Books, 1989

Powell, Jeff, *Bobby Moore: The Authorised Biography,* Everest Books, 1976

WEBSITES

McIlvanney, Hugh, *Remembering the life and football of Bobby Moore:* https://www.theguardian.com/sport/blog/2013/feb/22/vault-remembering-life-football-bobby-moore accessed 20 January, 2024

Parkinson, Gary, *Bobby Robson: One-on-One:* https://www.fourfourtwo.com/features/bobby-robson-one-one accessed 20 January, 2024

TELEVISION/RADIO SHOWS/PODCASTS

5 Live Sport, *A Tribute to Bobby Moore*, 2013

BBC Four, *Hero: The Bobby Moore Story*, 2006

BBC Two, *Bobby Moore – World Cup Hero*, 2002

BBC Radio 4 Extra, *Captain Fantastic – Bobby Moore*, 2002

Stuart Pearce

BOOKS

Pearce, Stuart, *Never Stop Dreaming: My Euro '96 Story*, Hodder & Stoughton, 2020

Pearce, Stuart, *Psycho: The Autobiography*, Headline, 2000

Robson, Bobby, *Against the Odds*, Stanley Paul, 1990

TELEVISION/RADIO SHOWS/PODCASTS

MOTD Top 10, S4 Ep 3, 2022

BBC Radio 5 Live, *Midnight Meets with Colin Murray*, 2022

Bobby Charlton

BOOKS

Charlton, Bobby, *My Manchester United Years: The Autobiography*, Headline, 2007

Powell, Jeff, *Bobby Moore: The Authorised Biography*, Everest Books, 1976

TELEVISION/RADIO SHOWS/PODCASTS

BBC One, *Sir Bobby Charlton at 80*, 2017

BBC Four, *Nation on Film: Munich Remembered*, 2008

BBC Two, *Kicking and Screaming*, 1994

David Beckham

BOOKS

Ferguson, Sir Alex, *Alex Ferguson: My Autobiography*, Hodder & Stoughton, 2013

Beckham, David, *David Beckham: My Side*, CollinsWillow, 2004

WEBSITES

Rice, Simon, *David Beckham retires: 'The time is right' to retire from football:* https://www.independent.co.uk/sport/football/news/david-beckham-retires-the-time-is-right-to-retire-from-football-8619336.html accessed 20 March, 2024

TELEVISION/RADIO SHOWS/PODCASTS

BBC Radio 4, *Desert Island Discs*, 2017

BBC One, *There's Only One David Beckham*, 2001

John Barnes

BOOKS

Barnes, John, *The Uncomfortable Truth About Racism*, Headline, 2021

Barrett, Norman S, *The Daily Telegraph Football Chronicle*, Carlton, 2003

Barnes, John, *John Barnes: The Autobiography*, Headline, 1999

Robson, Bobby, *Against the Odds*, Stanley Paul, 1990

WEBSITES

Barnes, John, *The Games That Changed My Life*: https://www.fourfourtwo.com/features/john-barnes-games-changed-my-life accessed 18 June, 2024

TELEVISION/RADIO SHOWS/PODCASTS

BBC Radio 4, *Saturday Live*, 2020

Paul Gascoigne

BOOKS

Gascoigne, Paul, *Gazza: My Story*, Headline, 2004

Hoddle, Glenn, *Glenn Hoddle: My 1998 World Cup Story*, Andre Deutsch, 1998

WEBSITES

Pilger, Sam, *Paul Gascoigne: One-on-One:* https://www.fourfourtwo.com/features/paul-gascoigne-one-one accessed 10 April, 2024

Gibbs, Tom, *Paul Gascoigne's Euro 96: joy, despair and a dentist's chair:* https://www.telegraph.co.uk/euro-2021/0/Paul-Gascoigne-Euro-96-joy-despair-dentist-chair/ accessed 10 April, 2024

TELEVISION/RADIO SHOWS/PODCASTS

BBC Two, *Gazza Episodes 1 & 2*, 2022

BBC Radio 5 Live, *Sportsweek*, 2011

BBC Two, *Natural Born Footballers*, 1995

Geoff Hurst

BOOKS

Hurst, Geoff, *1966 and All That: My Autobiography*, Headline, 2001

TELEVISION/RADIO SHOWS/PODCASTS

BBC Radio 5 Live, *Sportsweek*, 2011

BBC Two, *Match of Their Day*, 1999

Gary Lineker

BOOKS

Malam, Colin, *Gary Lineker: Strikingly Different*, Stanley Paul, 1993

WEBSITES

Lowe, Sid, *Gary Lineker, 'Diego was a mixed-up mess, but what a lovely guy':* https://www.theguardian.com/football/2021/oct/23/gary-lineker-diego-maradona-mixed-up-mess-lovely-guy accessed 15 May, 2024

Lineker, Gary, *The Games That Changed My Life:* https://www.fourfourtwo.com/features/gary-lineker-games-changed-my-life accessed 15 May, 2024

Lineker relives his first goal for England: https://www.thefa.com/news/2015/jun/05/gary-lineker-looks-back-ireland-1985 accessed 15 May, 2024

TELEVISION/RADIO SHOWS/PODCASTS

MOTD Top 10, *Cult Heroes,* 2024

BBC One, *Match of Their Day,* 1999

BBC Radio 4, *Desert Island Discs,* 1990

Harry Kane

WEBSITES

Kane, Harry, *Grassroots Story:* https://www.englandfootball.com/articles/2022/Nov/18/harry-kane-grassroots-story-20221118 accessed 18 July, 2024

Sessions, George, *Harry Kane: Former coach recognised England captain's big-game qualities at six years old:* https://www.independent.co.uk/sport/football/harry-kane-england-bobby-moore-wembley-kasper-schmeichel-b1881016.html accessed 18 July, 2024

Wilson, Bill, *Harry Kane and the Making of a Premier League football star:* https://www.bbc.co.uk/news/business-43512596 accessed 19 July 2024

Fordyce, Tom, *Harry Kane: The making of Tottenham & England striker:* https://www.bbc.co.uk/sport/football/36321045 accessed 19 July 2024

Baldi, Ryan, *Harry Kane: Tracking England Captain's Evolution:* https://www.bbc.co.uk/sport/football/57342918 accessed 20 July 2024

Kane, Harry, *The Games That Changed My Life:* https://www.fourfourtwo.com/news/i-really-might-not-be-where-i-am-today-without-that-performance-harry-kane-picks-the-games-that-changed-his-life accessed 20 July, 2024

Hytner, David, *Harry Kane's 'amazing journey' from Dublin swivel to Spurs' record scorer:* https://www.theguardian.com/football/2023/feb/06/harry-kanes-amazing-journey-from-dublin-swivel-to-spurs-record-scorer accessed 20 July, 2024

About the Author

Chris Bevan is a football journalist who specialises in ghost-writing opinion and analysis columns for the BBC Sport website working with television and radio pundits like Gary Lineker, Alan Shearer, Rio Ferdinand, Chris Sutton, Karen Bardsley, Ellen White and Micah Richards, and especially enjoys the chance to play 6-a-side with them whenever possible.

Ian Wright once described his left foot as 'cultured' but Chris's greatest sporting achievement on the pitch is probably being the last player to break his (right) leg at Highbury, in 2006.

He started his career covering Leyton Orient for the *Waltham Forest Guardian* and then became a freelance reporter for Sky Sports, the *Daily Mirror* and *Daily Express* before joining BBC Sport in 2000.

As well as being a keen football historian who loves taking a deep dive into statistics that show something you might otherwise have missed, Chris has a special passion for telling the stories of how young players survive different pitfalls to make their way in the game.

He has extensive experience of covering domestic and international football home and abroad, including attending the past four World Cups and three European Championships, and has also worked at 13 FA Cup finals at the new Wembley.

Chris has a BA (Hons) in English Literature from Middlesex University and lives in Manchester with his wife and two daughters, one of whom has already caught the football bug from their dad.

This is his first book, and you can follow him on X and Instagram at chrisbevan_bbc

ALSO IN THE SERIES

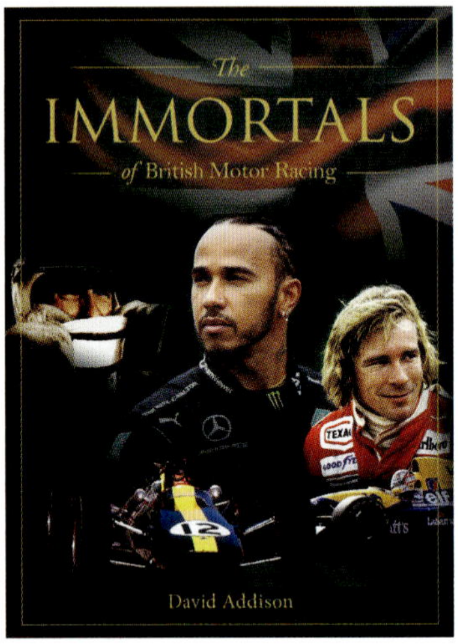

The Immortals of British Motor Racing
by David Addison
ISBN: 9781922662019

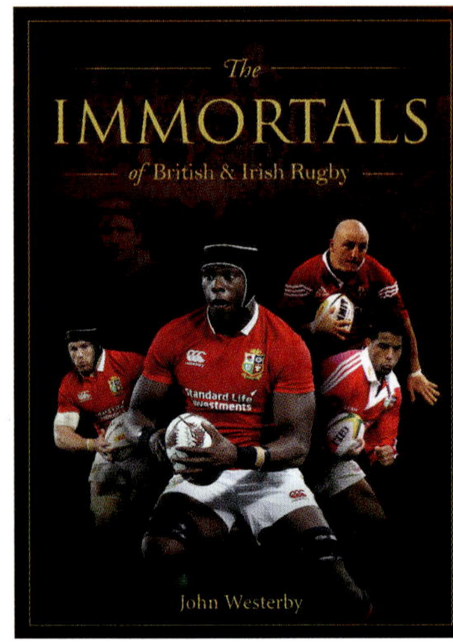

The Immortals of British & Irish Rugby Union
by John Westerby
ISBN: 9781922662064

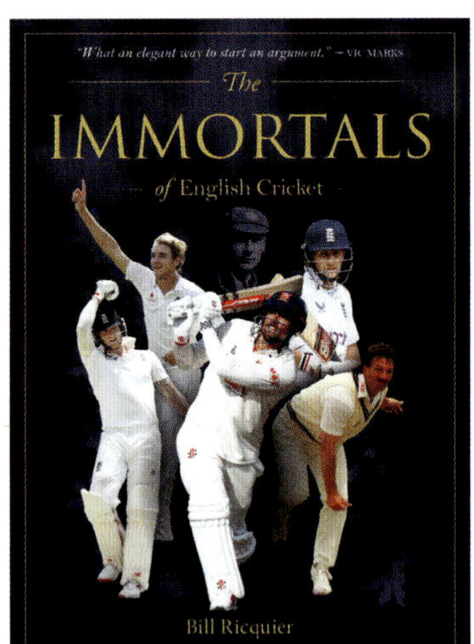

The Immortals of English Cricket
by Bill Ricquier
ISBN: 9781922662224

Available now from all good book stores.
geldingstreetpress.com

BOBBY MOORE · STUART PEARCE · BO
BARNES · PAUL GASCOIGNE · GEOFF
N BANKS · EDDIE HAPGOOD · BOBB
DAVID BECKHAM · JOHN BARNES ·
EKER · HARRY KANE · GORDON BAN
UART PEARCE · BOBBY CHARLTON ·
OIGNE · GEOFF HURST GARY LINEK
OOD · BOBBY MOORE · STUART PEA
· JOHN BARNES · PAUL GASCOIGNE
· GORDON BANKS · EDDIE HAPGOO
RLTON · DAVID BECKHAM · JOHN B
Y LINEKER · HARRY KANE · GORDO
TUART PEARCE · BOBBY CHARLTON ·
OIGNE · GEOFF HURST GARY LINEK
OOD · BOBBY MOORE · STUART PEA
· JOHN BARNES · PAUL GASCOIGNE
· GORDON BANKS · EDDIE HAPGOO
RLTON · DAVID BECKHAM · JOHN B
Y LINEKER · HARRY KANE · GORDO
TUART PEARCE · BOBBY CHARLTON ·
OIGNE · GEOFF HURST GARY LINEK
OOD · BOBBY MOORE · STUART PEA

RDON BANKS · EDDIE HAPGOOD · B
ARLTON · DAVID BECKHAM · JOHN
RY LINEKER · HARRY KANE · GORDO
UART PEARCE · BOBBY CHARLTON ·
SCOIGNE · GEOFF HURST GARY LIN
DIE HAPGOOD · BOBBY MOORE · STU
KHAM · JOHN BARNES · PAUL GASC
NE · GORDON BANKS · EDDIE HAPG
BBY CHARLTON · DAVID BECKHAM ·
RST GARY LINEKER · HARRY KANE ·
ORE · STUART PEARCE · BOBBY CHA
UL GASCOIGNE · GEOFF HURST GAR
DIE HAPGOOD · BOBBY MOORE · ST
KHAM · JOHN BARNES · PAUL GASC
NE · GORDON BANKS · EDDIE HAPG
BBY CHARLTON · DAVID BECKHAM
RST GARY LINEKER · HARRY KANE ·
ORE · STUART PEARCE · BOBBY CHA
UL GASCOIGNE · GEOFF HURST GAR
DIE HAPGOOD · BOBBY MOORE · ST
KHAM · JOHN BARNES · PAUL GASC
NE · GORDON BANKS · EDDIE HAPG